Systems and Software Verification

T0138044

Springer
Berlin
Heidelberg
New York
Barcelona
Hong Kong
London
Milan
Paris
Singapore
Tokyo

B. Bérard · M. Bidoit · A. Finkel · F. Laroussinie ·
A. Petit · L. Petrucci · Ph. Schnoebelen
with P. McKenzie

Systems and Software Verification

Model-Checking Techniques and Tools

With 67 Figures

Springer

Béatrice Bérard
Michel Bidoit
Alain Finkel
François Laroussinie
Antoine Petit
Laure Petrucci
Philippe Schnoebelen

Laboratoire Spécification et Vérification
CNRS, UMR 8643
Ecole Normale Supérieure de Cachan
61, avenue du Président Wilson
94235 Cachan Cedex, France
http://www.lsv.ens-cachan.fr/

Pierre McKenzie

Département d'Informatique
et Recherche Opérationnelle
Université de Montréal
CP 6128 succ Centre-Ville
Montréal QC H3C 3J7, Canada
http://www.iro.umontreal.ca/~mckenzie/

Translated with the help of Pierre McKenzie, Université de Montréal

Updated version of the French language edition:
"Vérification de logiciels. Techniques et outils du model-checking",
coordonné par Philippe Schnoebelen
Copyright © Vuibert, Paris, 1999
Tous droits réservés

Library of Congress Cataloging-in-Publication Data applied for
Die Deutsche Bibliothek – CIP-Einheitsaufnahme

Systems and software verification: model-checking techniques and tools / Bérard ... –
Berlin; Heidelberg; New York; Barcelona; Hong Kong; London; Milan; Paris; Singapore; Tokyo:
Springer, 2001

ACM Computing Classification (1998): D.2.4, D.2, D.4.5, F.3.1–2, F.4.1, G.4, I.2.2

ISBN 978-3-642-07478-3

Springer-Verlag Berlin Heidelberg New York
a member of Springer Science+Business Media
http://www.springer.de

© Springer-Verlag Berlin Heidelberg 2001
Softcover reprint of the hardcover 1st edition 2001

Cover design: KünkelLopka, Heidelberg

Printed on acid-free paper

Foreword

One testament to the maturing of a research field is the adoption of its techniques in industrial practice; another is the emergence of textbooks. According to both signs, research in model checking is now entering its mature phase, some twenty years after almost entirely theoretical beginnings. It has been an exciting twenty years, which have seen the research focus evolve, like the business plan of a successful enterprise, from a dream of automatic program verification to a reality of computer-aided design debugging.

Those who have participated in significant hardware designs or embedded software projects have experienced that the system complexity, and hence the likely number of design errors, grows exponentially with the number of interacting system components. Furthermore, traditional debugging and validation techniques, based on simulation and testing, are woefully inadequate for detecting errors in highly concurrent designs. It is therefore in such applications that model-checking-based techniques, despite their limitations in the face of the exponential complexity growth, are making inroads into the design flow and the supporting software tools.

This monograph, with its emphasis on skills, craft, and tools, will be of particular value, first, to the practitioner of formal verification, and second, as a textbook for courses on formal verification that —as, I believe, all courses on formal verification should— contain a significant experimental component. The selected model-checking tools are available to the public, free of charge, and are suitable for use in the classroom. The reader is exposed to a broad mix of different tools, from widely used, mature software to experimental tools at the research frontier, including programs for model checking real-time and hybrid systems. In this way, the book succeeds in providing both: a survey of established techniques in model checking, as well as a glimpse at state-of-the-art research.

Berkeley, February 2001   *Thomas A. Henzinger*

Preface

This book is an introduction to *model checking*, a technique for automatic verification of software and reactive systems. Model checking was invented more than twenty years ago. It was first developed by academic research teams and has more recently been introduced in specialized industrial units. It has now proven to be a successful method, frequently used to uncover well-hidden bugs in sizeable industrial cases. Numerous studies are still in progress, both to extend the area covered by this technique and to increase its efficiency. This leads us to believe that its industrial applications will grow significantly in the next few years.

The book contains the basic elements required for understanding model checking and is intended both as a textbook for undergraduate courses in computer science and as a reference for professional engineers. It may also be of interest to researchers, lecturers or PhD students wishing to prepare a talk or an overview on the subject. To increase his theoretical knowledge on model checking, the reader is invited to consult the excellent monograph *Model Checking* (MIT Press), by Clarke, Grumberg and Peled, which had not yet been published when the French edition of this book appeared.

The first part of the book presents the fundamental principles underlying model checking. The second part considers the problem of specification in more detail. It provides some help for the design of temporal logic formulae to express classes of properties, which are widely used in practice. The third part describes, from a user's point of view, some significant model checkers freely available in the academic world. All of them have been used by the authors in the course of their industrial collaborations.

This book was written by French researchers from *Laboratoire Spécification et Vérification* (LSV), a joint laboratory of École Normale Supérieure de Cachan and Centre National de la Recherche Scientifique. It is a revised translation of *Vérification de logiciels : Techniques et outils du model-checking*, (Vuibert, 1999), a former French undergraduate/graduate textbook co-ordinated by Philippe Schnoebelen and written by Béatrice Bérard, Michel Bidoit, François Laroussinie, Antoine Petit and Philippe Schnoebelen, with the help of Gérard Cécé, Catherine Dufourd, Alain Finkel, Laure Petrucci and Grégoire Sutre. The French book was itself derived from a collaboration between the French Electricity Company (EDF) and the LSV.

Acknowledgements. Gérard Cécé, Roopa Chauhan, Sandrine Couffin, Catherine Dufourd, Paul Gastin, Jean Goubault-Larrecq, Jean-Michel Hufflen, Amélie Josselin, Pierre McKenzie, Christine Pellen, Sophie Pinchinat, Marie-Pierre Ponpon, Jérôme Ryckbosch and Grégoire Sutre read the first versions of the book. Their numerous remarks and suggestions were invaluable to the production of the final version.

Contents

Part III. Some Tools

Part I

Principles and Techniques

Introduction

This first part describes the concepts underlying the techniques of model checking. A reader confronted with verification questions will find here just enough theory to be able to assess the relevance of the various tools, to understand the reasons behind their limitations and strengths, and to choose the approach concretely best suited for his/her verification task.

The following are described in turn:

- **automata** which form the basis of the operational models used to specify the behavior of the systems to be validated;
- **temporal logic** and its use in specifying properties;
- **model checking** based on explicit enumeration;
- **symbolic model checking** based on binary decision trees;
- **timed automata** and their related methods.

Chapter 1, "Automata", is the easiest to follow. The notions discussed there are in all likelihood already familiar and they constitute an essential prerequisite. Chapters 2, 3 and 4 form a logical sequence. Chapter 5 is in large part independent.

The concepts presented in the first two chapters are fundamental. They are used throughout the book.

1. Automata

As mentioned in the foreword, model checking consists in verifying some properties of the *model* of a system. Before any checking can begin, one is thus confronted with the task of modeling the system under study. To be honest, we stress that this modeling step is difficult, and yet crucial to the relevance of the results subsequently obtained. No universal method exists to model a system: modeling is a challenging task best performed by qualified engineers enlightened with a good grasp of both the physical reality and the applicable mathematical or computer models. Alternatively, a pre-modeling step involving mixed teams of modeling experts and "area" specialists is advisable. This chapter does not claim to provide a fool-proof modeling method (an otherwise over-ambitious goal to say the least). We will, rather more humbly, describe a general model which serves as a basis, under a guise or another, for most model checking methods. Using toy examples in this chapter, we will illustrate how this general model is used to represent objects or "real-life" systems.

1.1 Introductory Examples

The systems best suited for verification by model checking techniques are those that are easily modeled by (finite) automata. Briefly put, an automaton is a machine evolving from one *state* to another under the action of *transitions*. For example, a digital watch can be represented by an automaton in which each state represents the current hour and minutes (we neglect the seconds), there are thus $24 \times 60 = 1440$ possible states, and one transition links any pair of states representing times one minute apart.

An automaton (or part of an automaton) is often depicted by drawing each state as a circle and each transition as an arrow (see figure 1.1). An incoming arrow without origin identifies the initial state.

The availability of such graphical representations is one of the benefits of automata-based formalisms. These representations provide invaluable support for building our understanding of a system's operation.

Another example (this one completely representable, see figure 1.2) is that of a modulo 3 counter, whose automaton will be denoted $\mathcal{A}_{c3}$ (the watch above could be viewed as some sort of modulo 1440 counter). The states

Fig. 1.1. A model of a watch

of $\mathcal{A}_{c3}$ correspond to the possible counter values. Its transitions reflect the possible actions on the counter. In this example we restrict our operations to increments (inc) and decrements (dec).

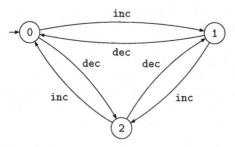

Fig. 1.2. $\mathcal{A}_{c3}$: a modulo 3 counter

In the same way, an integer variable can be modeled by an automaton having an infinite number of states (one per possible value) and having one transition per basic operation allowed on this variable (surely increment/decrement by 1, but maybe also a sign change or the squaring operation). Although there exist model checking techniques dealing with restricted classes of automata with infinitely many states, such techniques will only be mentioned indirectly in this book. Accordingly, we assume from here onwards that an automaton has a finite number of states and transitions, unless we specifically mention otherwise.

Now consider a slightly more elaborate example, that of a digicode such as those which control the opening of offices or building doors. The door opens upon the keying in of the correct character sequence, irrespective (in the simple digicode modeled here) of any possible incorrect initial attempt. To keep things simple, we assume that 3 keys, A, B and C, are available, and that the door opens whenever ABA is keyed in. The resulting digicode can be modeled by the 4-state and 9-transition automaton depicted on figure 1.3. Note how a single arrow in the figure sometimes represents two transitions having the same origin and the same end point (for example going from 3 to 1, or from 1 to 1), one labelled B and the other labelled C.

The digicode example will serve to illustrate two fundamental notions, that of an *execution* and that of an *execution tree* of the system model. An execution is a sequence of states describing one possible evolution of the system. Thus 1121, 12234 and 112312234 are executions of the digicode. In

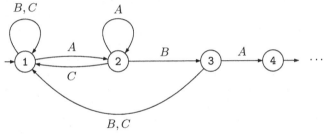

Fig. 1.3. A model of a digicode

some cases, it is useful to spell out the transition which allows one to go from a state to the next (in the execution 1121 we cannot tell which letter was keyed in when the state went from 1 to 1), though we will seldom require this extra information, which adds in fact no conceptual difficulty and which is left out of most work related to model checking.

We will also concern ourselves with the set of all possible executions of the system. One way to describe this set would be to "rank" the executions in some order (for example in increasing order of length). The digicode would then yield

1
11, 12
111, 112, 121, 122, 123
1111, 1112, 1121, 1122, 1123, 1211, 1212, 1221, 1222, 1223, 1231, 1234
. . .

For reasons which will become clear, we prefer to organize the set of executions in the form of a *tree*. In Computer Science, a tree is drawn with its root at the top. Here the root is the initial state 1 and its children are all the states accessible in one step (we speak of *immediate successors*) from the root, namely 1 and 2 in our example. We start over again with the nodes 1 and 2 just created, which respectively have two children labelled 1 and 2, and three children labelled 1, 2 and 3. We ultimately obtain a representation, most often infinite, of the set of system executions (see figure 1.4).

Since our goal is to verify system properties, or more accurately, to verify system model properties, we will associate with each automaton state a number of elementary properties which we know are satisfied. Consider for example the "door is open" property; it holds in state 4 and it fails in states 1, 2 and 3. In our digicode example, our main interest is the knowledge that:

1. If the door opens (if an execution reaches state 4), then A, B, A were the last three letters keyed in, in that order.
2. Keying in any sequence of letters ending in ABA opens the door (that is, defines an execution leading to state 4).

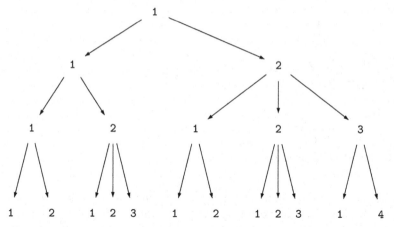

Fig. 1.4. The beginning of the execution tree of the digicode

An essential step in the modeling process is the construction of an automaton, representing the system under consideration, in which we can associate with each state some elementary properties which we know to be true or false. We must later be able to express, using these elementary properties, the more "complicated" properties which we would really like our system to satisfy. The way in which the "complicated" properties are expressed using the elementary properties depends on the *logic* we use. It precisely is the goal of the next chapter to define these logics. To distinguish the elementary properties from the more complicated, we speak of *(atomic) propositions* when referring to elementary properties, true or false in a given state.

Here we merely sketch intuitive ideas. In our ongoing example, we might be led to define the elementary properties:

P_A: an A has just been keyed in;
P_B: a B has just been keyed in;
P_C: a C has just been keyed in.

The P_A property holds in states 2 and 4, P_B holds in state 3 alone (indeed not in state 1, which could also have been accessed by keying in C), and P_C holds in no state.

Let us also define the following properties:

$pred_2$: the preceding state in an execution is 2;
$pred_3$: the preceding state in an execution is 3.

Hence $pred_2$ holds in state 3 alone and $pred_3$ holds in state 4 alone. Now consider an execution which results in an open door, that is, an execution ending in state 4. Since $pred_3$ holds in state 4, this execution must end with the sequence 3 4. But $pred_2$ holds in state 3, hence in fact the execution ends with the sequence 2 3 4. Since P_A holds in states 2 and 4 and P_B holds in state 3, we conclude that the last three letters keyed in were A, B, A in that order.

We have thus "proved" one of the two required properties: if the door opens, then the "correct" sequence of letters was keyed in. The other property is obtained from the elementary properties in an analogous manner.

Model checking precisely consists of techniques making it possible to automatically perform such verifications.

1.2 A Few Definitions

We will now briefly define the notions introduced above. What we have referred to as an *automaton* draws characteristics from the finite automata of language theory, as well as from the notions of *Kripke structures* and *transition systems* used in other areas.

Automata. A set $Prop = \{P_1, \ldots\}$ of elementary propositions (properties) is given. An automaton is a tuple $\mathcal{A} = \langle Q, E, T, q_0, l \rangle$ in which

- Q is a finite set of states;
- E is the finite set of transition labels;
- $T \subseteq Q \times E \times Q$ is the set of transitions;
- q_0 is the initial state of the automaton;
- l is the mapping which associates with each state of Q the finite set of elementary properties which hold in that state.

If we restrict our attention to the four visible states on figure 1.3, the modeling of the digicode corresponds to the following formal automaton definition:

$$Q=\{1,2,3,4\} \;; \qquad T=\{(1,A,2),(1,B,1),(1,C,1),$$
$$E=\{A,B,C\} \;; \qquad\quad (2,A,2),(2,B,3),(2,C,1),$$
$$q_0=1 \;; \qquad\qquad\quad (3,A,4),(3,B,1),(3,C,1)\} \;;$$

$$l=\begin{cases} 1 \mapsto \emptyset \;; \\ 2 \mapsto \{P_A\} \;; \\ 3 \mapsto \{P_B, \text{pred}_2\} \;; \\ 4 \mapsto \{P_A, \text{pred}_3\}. \end{cases}$$

Graphical representation. Note that figure 1.3 does not include all the information available in the tuple $\langle Q, E, T, q_0, l \rangle$ just spelled out. Indeed, the labelling of the states by their atomic propositions was not depicted, in order to keep the original diagram simple. We will henceforth often represent automata with atomic propositions appearing within the states verifying them. Occasionally, for lack of space, we will omit some propositions, or some state names. See figure 1.5 for a complete representation of the digicode example.

Similarly, we will occasionally omit, or even fail to consider, the transition labels [1], for instance when these are not relevant, as in the watch example (figure 1.1).

---

[1] And we will then view T as a subset of $Q \times Q$.

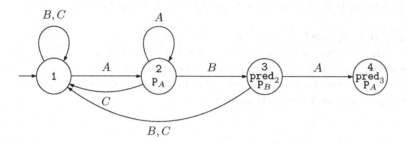

Fig. 1.5. The digicode with its atomic propositions

Formal definition of behavior. A *path* of an automaton $\mathcal{A}$ is simply a sequence σ, finite or infinite, of transitions (q_i, e_i, q_i') of $\mathcal{A}$ which follow each other, that is, such that $q_i' = q_{i+1}$ for each i. We often label such a sequence in the form $q_1 \xrightarrow{e_1} q_2 \xrightarrow{e_2} q_3 \xrightarrow{e_3} \cdots$. For example, "$3 \xrightarrow{B} 1 \xrightarrow{A} 2 \xrightarrow{A} 2$" is a path in the digicode (see figure 1.5).

The *length* of a path σ, denoted $|\sigma|$, is its potentially infinite number of transitions: $|\sigma| \in \mathbb{N} \cup \{\omega\}$ (where $\mathbb{N}$ denotes the set of natural numbers and ω denotes infinity). The *ith state* of σ, written $\sigma(i)$, is the state q_i reached after i transitions. The latter is defined only if $i < |\sigma|$.

A *partial execution* of $\mathcal{A}$ is a path starting from the initial state q_0. For example "$1 \xrightarrow{A} 2 \xrightarrow{A} 2 \xrightarrow{B} 3$" is a partial execution of the digicode.

A *complete execution* is an execution which is *maximal*, that is, which cannot be extended. It is thus either infinite, or it ends in a state q_n out of which no transition of the automaton under consideration is possible (in this case we can speak of a *deadlock*).

When we speak of an *execution* without qualifiers, we generally refer to a complete execution. Occasionally we will vary the initial state; we would indicate this by referring to an "execution out of ...".

It is the complete executions which are the true behaviors of an automaton; these relate to the liveness assumption according to which an automaton always eventually performs yet another transition. (Note that our modeling examples, starting with the watch, often relied on this hypothesis).

Giving a formal definition for an execution tree would be too cumbersome and tedious, and would not contribute to our discussion. We will thus be content with our informal treatment of that notion, as per our digicode example above.

To conclude these definitions, we introduce the notion of a *reachable* state. A state is said to be reachable if it appears in the execution tree of the automaton, or in other words, if there exists at least one execution in which it appears. Until now, all the states of all the automata that we considered were reachable. We will see later that this is not always the case.

1.3 A Printer Manager

Consider another example, that of a printer shared by two users. Suppose that the result of modeling this manager is the finite automaton given by figure 1.6.

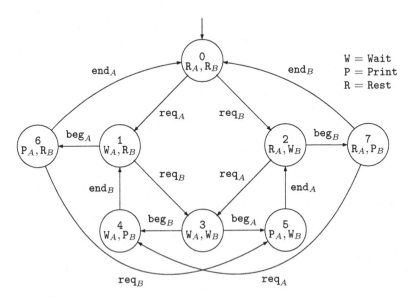

Fig. 1.6. A printer manager

Obviously, most important is the "physical" meaning of the various actions or propositions. The req_A action is a print request by user A. The beg_A action is a message from the printer indicating the start of the print job requested by user A. The end_A action is a message from the printer indicating the end of the print job requested by A. The req_B, beg_B and end_B actions are the corresponding printing steps originating from user B. The atomic propositions correspond to the following physical facts:

W_A: a request by user A has not yet been processed (user A "is waiting");
W_B: a request by user B has not yet been processed;
P_A: the printer is printing a document for user A;
P_B: the printer is printing a document for user B;
R_A: no request from user A is pending (user A is at "rest");
R_B: no request from user B is pending.

Formally, the print manager is thus modeled by the finite automaton $\mathcal{A} = \langle Q, E, T, q_0, l \rangle$ with:

$Q = \{0, 1, 2, 3, 4, 5, 6, 7\}$;

$E = \{\text{req}_A, \text{req}_B, \text{beg}_A, \text{beg}_B, \text{end}_A, \text{end}_B\}$;

$q_0 = 0$;

$T = \{(0, \text{req}_A, 1), (0, \text{req}_B, 2), (1, \text{req}_B, 3), (1, \text{beg}_A, 6), (2, \text{req}_A, 3),$
$\qquad (2, \text{beg}_B, 7), (3, \text{beg}_A, 5), (3, \text{beg}_B, 4), (4, \text{end}_B, 1), (5, \text{end}_A, 2),$
$\qquad (6, \text{end}_A, 0), (6, \text{req}_B, 5), (7, \text{end}_B, 0), (7, \text{req}_A, 4)\}$;

$$l = \begin{cases} 0 \mapsto \{R_A, R_B\}, & 1 \mapsto \{W_A, R_B\}, \\ 2 \mapsto \{R_A, W_B\}, & 3 \mapsto \{W_A, W_B\}, \\ 4 \mapsto \{W_A, P_B\}, & 5 \mapsto \{P_A, W_B\}, \\ 6 \mapsto \{P_A, R_B\}, & 7 \mapsto \{R_A, P_B\}. \end{cases}$$

Now that the printer manager is completely modeled, we can study its properties (more accurately, properties of its model). For example, we would undoubtedly wish to prove that any printing operation is preceded by a print request. Given the above propositions, this translates, for user A, into:

1. In any execution, any state in which P_A holds is preceded by a state in which the proposition W_A holds.
   Similarly, we would like to check that any print request is ultimately satisfied, which, for user A, translates into:
2. In any execution, any state in which W_A holds is followed (possibly not immediately) by a state in which the proposition P_A holds.

Model checking techniques allow us to prove automatically that property 1 is satisfied (which is also easily done "by hand" for such a simple example).

These techniques are also capable of identifying a counter-example witnessing the failure of property 2. It suffices, for example, to consider the execution 0 1 3 4 1 3 4 1 3 4 1 3 4 1 ... (where we have omitted the labels). This print manager is thus not "*fair*". Because it does not process requests in the order in which these were issued, the print manager can postpone printing a document indefinitely !

1.4 A Few More Variables

When modeling real-life systems, it is often convenient to let automata manipulate *state variables*. We then hit upon the classical dichotomy between control and data: the "states+transitions" constructs of an automaton represent the control, and the variables represent the data.

Most often, the variables of an automaton only assume a finite number of values, either because this is a feature of the system being modeled, or because this restriction was added on purpose (for example, to make possible the use of a model checking tool). Even if, from a theoretical viewpoint, variables which take only finitely many values could themselves be modeled by automata [2], it is more convenient to consider them explicitly.

Thus, in the digicode example, suppose that we have to count the number of mistakes from the user. For this, we would add an integer variable ctr, with initial value 0, to accumulate the number of mistakes. An automaton interacts with variables in two ways:

Assignments: a transition can modify the value of one (or more) variable(s). Hence in the digicode, transitions corresponding to a mistake, that is, all transitions except $(1, A, 2)$, $(2, B, 3)$ et $(3, A, 4)$, would increase the counter.

Guards: a transition can be *guarded* by a condition on the variables. This means that the transition cannot occur unless the condition on the variables holds.

Back to the digicode again, if we wished to tolerate no more than three mistakes from the user, the transitions corresponding to a mistake $(1, B, 1)$, $(1, C, 1)$, $(2, C, 1)$, etc. would be guarded by the condition ctr < 3. We then refine the system by adding an alarm which sounds when four mistakes are detected. We create a new state err and three transitions from 1 to err, 2 to err and 3 to err guarded by the condition ctr $= 3$.

var ctr : int ;

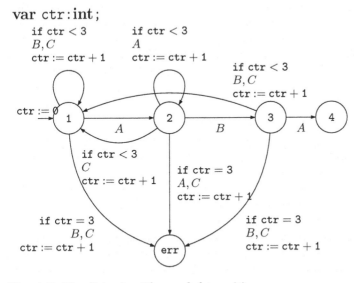

Fig. 1.7. The digicode with guarded transitions

---

[2] For example, the $\mathcal{A}_{c3}$ counter from figure 1.2 could represent a variable storing an integer modulo 3. As needed, the counter could be enriched with further transitions corresponding to new operations on the variables: zero resets, etc.

Graphical representation. The digicode automaton with the variable `ctr` is depicted on figure 1.7. The transitions are equipped with guards and variable updates according to a well-established graphical convention: the guards are preceded by the keyword `if`, then come the transition labels, and in the end come the assignments. To simplify, we omit both the "always true" guards, which appear on unconditional transitions, and the empty assignments, which modify no variable.

Unfolding. It is often necessary, in order to apply model checking methods for instance, to *unfold* the behavior of an automaton with variables into a state graph in which the possible transitions (and those only) appear and the configurations are clearly marked. We will retain the "automaton" terminology for this unfolded system, even if the more technical term *transition system* is often used in the literature. We will speak of the unfolded automaton associated with (the automaton) $\mathcal{A}$.

The states of the unfolded automaton are called *global states*. They have many components: the state corresponding to the "small" original automaton $\mathcal{A}$, and a component for each variable, giving its value. Rather than make this definition formal, we will illustrate how it works using the example of the digicode with the error counter. After unfolding, we obtain the automaton of figure 1.8.

Note that the transitions are no longer guarded. Since we explicitly know the value of the counter in each state, we know whether a guarded transition is possible or not (in the latter case, there is simply no transition) without the need to carry the guards around.

Note also that there are no assignments on the transitions. Since we know the value of the counter in each state, a transition leads directly to the global state in which the new counter value, resulting from a potential update by a transition, appears.

In a global state such as $\langle 1, \mathtt{ctr} = 0 \rangle$, we say that 1 is the *control state*. Indeed, the control state is the component which identifies a "state" of the automaton prior to its unfolding. The control state determines in large part the relevant transitions, notwithstanding the effect, via the guards, of the current values of the variables.

1.5 Synchronized Product

The discussion above showed how simple objects (a counter, a digicode, a printer manager, etc.) are modeled by finite automata. When we deal with real-life programs or systems, these are often broken up into modules or subsystems. To build a model of the overall system, it is therefore natural to first model the system components. Then, the global automaton is obtained from the component automata by having them cooperate.

There are many ways of achieving this cooperation – we say *synchronization* – between automata. Here we briefly describe the main methods. Note

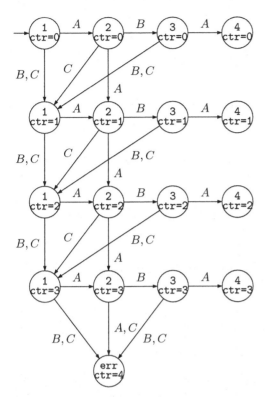

Fig. 1.8. The digicode with error counting

that an automaton representing the overall system often has so many states that constructing it directly is next to impossible. We speak of *state explosion*. It is not uncommon to quickly exceed a billion states, which corresponds to the memory available on standard computers.

An example without synchronization. The simplest situation is when the system can be broken up into components which *do not interact with each other*. The global automaton is then the *cartesian product* of the automata representing the components, that is, a (global) state is in fact a vector made up of the different component states (the local states).

For example, to model a system made up of a counter modulo 2, a counter modulo 3 and a counter modulo 4, we will use the automaton $\mathcal{A}_{c3}$ encountered earlier (see figure 1.2) and we will build the automata $\mathcal{A}_{c2}$ and $\mathcal{A}_{c4}$ in a similar way. Our final system will be made up of three automata having 2, 3 and 4 states respectively.

The global system automaton, denoted $\mathcal{A}_{ccc}$, then has $2 \times 3 \times 4 = 24$ states. These states are represented on figure 1.9, where we have used perspective to illustrate how each state consists of three distinct components which are in

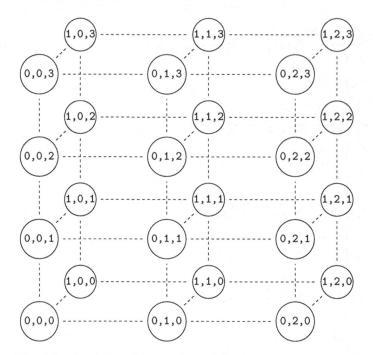

Fig. 1.9. The states of the product of the three counters

fact individual counters. The states of the counters modulo 2, 3 and 4 vary respectively with the depth, width and height.

We have yet to specify the transitions between these 24 states. These are obtained in fact from the individual counters. If no synchronization is desired, then each component in each state (that is, each individual counter) can be decremented, incremented, or left unchanged. This yields $3 \times 3 \times 3 = 27$ possible choices.

Note that for an individual counter, remaining unchanged corresponds to none of the transitions from figure 1.2. This new possibility is introduced for the purpose of describing what a counter does when a different counter evolves independently: the counter does nothing! For that reason, we choose to ignore, among the 27 possibilities, those in which no individual counter evolves. There remain 26 possible transitions from each state, hence $24 \times 26 = 624$ transitions in the global automaton.

Figure 1.10 depicts some of the transitions out of the initial state 0,0,0. Not to overload the diagram, we have only included the transitions corresponding to one (or more) increments, and suppressed any reference to decrements. In this way, there remain $2 \times 2 \times 2 - 1 = 7$ transitions to be represented, down from 26. The transition from 0,0,0 to 0,1,1 is labelled "-,inc,inc" to indicate that the first component does nothing (denoted -) and that the other two components each perform an inc transition.

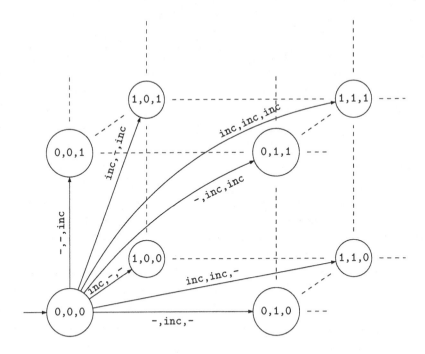

Fig. 1.10. A few transitions of the product of the three counters

An example with synchronization. If we now wish to synchronize the three counters, many variants are possible (the choice of one or the other of course depends on the nature of the problem to be modeled). For example, we can couple our three counters and forbid them from either evolving independently or remaining unchanged. Then, only two transitions, labelled "inc,inc,inc" and "dec,dec,dec", would leave each state, and only some states would be reachable.

Another possibility, quite opposite, is to decouple the counters and to allow updates in only one of the counters at a time. The transitions out of each state would be those which update a single counter, for example "-,-,inc", and those which decrement a single counter. An automaton with $24 \times 3 \times 2$ transitions would result. We can imagine an intermediate situation in which the first two counters increase simultaneously or the last two decrease simultaneously.

All these options are easily expressed in a common formal setting, called the synchronized product of automata and introduced by Arnold and Nivat [AN82, Arn92].

Synchronized product. Let us consider a family of n automata, $\forall i \in \{1, \ldots, n\}$ $\mathcal{A}_i = \langle Q_i, E_i, T_i, q_{0,i}, l_i \rangle$, and introduce a new label $'-'$ to represent the fictitious action "do nothing" for any automaton which remains inactive during a global transition of the set of components.

The *cartesian product* $\mathcal{A}_1 \times \cdots \times \mathcal{A}_n$ of these automata is simply the automaton $\mathcal{A} = \langle Q, E, T, q_0, l \rangle$ with:

- $Q = Q_1 \times \cdots \times Q_n$;
- $E = \prod_{1 \leq i \leq n}(E_i \cup \{-\})$;
- $T = \left\{ \begin{array}{l} ((q_1, \ldots, q_n), (e_1, \ldots, e_n), (q'_1, \ldots, q'_n)) \mid \text{ for all } i, \\ e_i = '-' \text{ and } q'_i = q_i, \text{ or } e_i \neq '-' \text{ and } (q_i, e_i, q'_i) \in T_i \end{array} \right\}$;
- $q_0 = (q_{0,1}, \ldots, q_{0,n})$;
- $l((q_1, \ldots, q_n)) = \bigcup_{1 \leq i \leq n} l_i(q_i)$.

Hence, in a cartesian product, each component $\mathcal{A}_i$ may, in a transition, either do nothing (fictitious action $'-'$) or perform a "local" transition. There is no synchronization requirement whatsoever between the various components. Moreover, the cartesian product contains transitions in which all components "do nothing" (perform $'-'$).

To synchronize the components, we will restrict the transitions allowed in the cartesian product. We thus define a *synchronization set*:

$$\text{Sync} \subseteq \prod_{1 \leq i \leq n} (E_i \cup \{-\}).$$

Sync indicates, among the labels of the cartesian product, those which really correspond to a synchronization (they are *permitted*) and those which do not (they are *forbidden* and do not appear in the resulting automaton).

For example, if we wish to strongly couple the 3 counters as in our earlier example, we can define as synchronization set:

$$\text{Sync} = \{(\texttt{inc}, \texttt{inc}, \texttt{inc}), (\texttt{dec}, \texttt{dec}, \texttt{dec})\}$$

and denote by $\mathcal{A}_{\texttt{ccc}}^{\texttt{coupl}}$ the resulting automaton (figure 1.11).

A synchronized product is thus given by the family of components automata and the synchronization set. That is, an execution of the synchronized product is an execution of the cartesian product in which all transitions are labelled by an element from Sync. The synchronized product can thus be defined by replacing, in the direct product definition, the clause which specifies the set of transitions, by:

$$T = \left\{ \begin{array}{l} ((q_1, \ldots, q_n), (e_1, \ldots, e_n), (q'_1, \ldots, q'_n)) \mid (e_1, \ldots, e_n) \in \text{Sync} \\ \text{and } \forall i,\ e_i = '-' \text{ and } q'_i = q_i, \text{ or } e_i \neq '-' \text{ and } (q_i, e_i, q'_i) \in T_i \end{array} \right\}.$$

In this book, we sometimes use the notation $\mathcal{A}_1 \parallel \ldots \parallel \mathcal{A}_n$ for products of automata. The underlying synchronization set must then be specified separately (or remain implicit).

Relabelling. Once a complicated automaton is constructed as a synchronization of many smaller automata representing subsystems, it is customary to *replace* some labels in the product automaton. For example, in the strongly coupled version of our counters product, we prefer to tersely write inc instead of the redundant (inc,inc,inc).

In other situations the motivation is different. For example, we may no longer wish to distinguish between labels used only for the purpose of synchronizing their transitions, and whose identity is irrelevant once the global product is obtained.

In this book, we omit the formal (though natural, but uninformative) definitions of such relabelling operations. We will use relabelling freely nonetheless.

Reachable states. Deciding if some state in a synchronized product is reachable is far from obvious. Reachability of course heavily depends on the accompanying synchronization constraints. For instance, in the example of the three counters, only 12 states are reachable if we force the three counters to evolve simultaneously. If we relax this synchronization by freeing the third counter, all 24 states again become reachable. However, if the second counter is freed instead, then the reachable states are those whose first and third components are given by the pairs $(0,0)$, $(1,1)$, $(0,2)$ and $(1,3)$. This yields 12 reachable states.

Figure 1.11 depicts the strongly coupled product of our three counters when only the states reachable from the initial state are considered, together with the transitions linking these states. Each transition is a (triple) increment or a (triple) decrement.

Obviously, a simpler way to visualize the result calls for a spatial rearrangement of the automaton: figure 1.12 makes plain that the strongly coupled product behaves as a modulo 12 counter. The non-reachable states are depicted using dotted lines. They also exhibit the behavior of a modulo 12 counter.

In the sequel, we will call *reachability graph* the automaton obtained (from a given automaton) by deleting the non-reachable states. This is the only part of the given automaton truly relevant to a description of its behavior. For example, the reachability graph of $\mathcal{A}_{ccc}^{coupl}$ is obtained by deleting anything drawn in dotted lines on figure 1.12.

Reachable states and verification. When a system has to be verified, it often turns out that the property we are interested in is simply expressible in terms of reachability (chapter 6 is devoted to reachability properties).

For example, in the case of a printer manager built as a synchronized product, we would require that no state in which both users are printing simultaneously is reachable.

To address such questions, a tool able to construct the reachability graph of synchronized products of automata would be most useful. Such tools are described in the third part of this book.

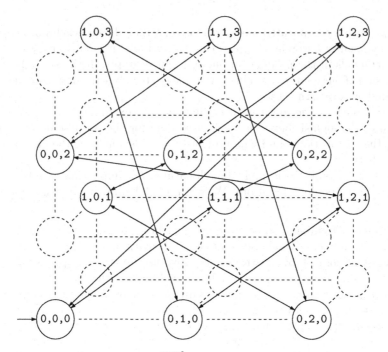

Fig. 1.11. The automaton $\mathcal{A}_{ccc}^{coupl}$ restricted to reachable states

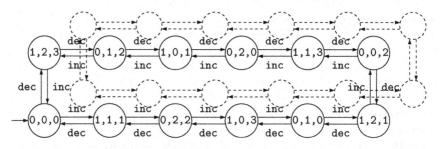

Fig. 1.12. The rearranged automaton $\mathcal{A}_{ccc}^{coupl}$

We earlier alluded to the difficulty of determining whether a state in a synchronized product is reachable. The problem is in fact very combinatorial in nature. In general, as explained later, any method will more or less construct (or explore) the reachability graph (section 6.3). The size of this graph can be overwhelming. Let the automata $\mathcal{A}_1$, ..., $\mathcal{A}_p$ have $n_1, \ldots, n_p$ states respectively. Their synchronized product will involve a number of states of order $n_1 \times n_2 \times \ldots \times n_p$ which grows very quickly, exponentially in p. This is the *state explosion problem*, to be encountered again in section 3.3.

When an automaton with variables is unfolded, the number of global states in the resulting global automaton is infinite if the variables have an infinite range, and this number is potentially exponential if the variables are bounded.

A special case, interesting from a theoretical point of view and important in practice, concerns *Petri nets*. Petri nets are operational models well suited for expressing parallel systems (the interested reader is referred to [VC92] for example).

In the framework of this book, Petri nets can either be viewed as strengthened synchronized automata permitting the dynamic creation of parallel components, or as automata juggling with integer counters through the use of a restricted set of primitives. Chapter 14 describes a tool specifically tailored for Petri nets.

A famous result of Kosaraju and Mayr [Kos82, May84] shows that, in Petri nets, reachability of a state is decidable even when the reachability set is infinite (we refer the interested reader to the very lucid [Reu89]).

1.6 Synchronization by Message Passing

A special case of synchronized product appears in the message passing framework. Among transition labels, we distinguish those associated with emitting a message m, denoted !m and those associated with the reception of this message, denoted ?m. In the synchronized product, only the transitions in which a given emission is executed simultaneously with the corresponding reception will be permitted.

A smallish elevator. To illustrate these notions, consider an elevator in a three-story building. We will model this elevator by singling out the following components:

the cabin which goes up and down depending on the current floor and on the commands of the elevator controller;

three doors (one per floor) which open and close according to the commands of the controller;

a controller which commands the three doors and the cabin.

Our model is rather coarse, and it does not try to account for the elevator requests from the three floors (that is, from the world outside the system).

We have yet to define our five automata. The cabin states (see figure 1.13) correspond to the three floors. The cabin receives instructions to "go up" or to "go down" (up and down messages) and it takes them into account when changing state. Note that our model silently accepts all commands but actually executes only those commands which are physically possible. For example, down has no effect when the cabin is on the ground floor (numbered zero).

The states of a door (see figure 1.14) are simply O for "open", and C for "closed". Here as well, the controller commands are always accepted, even when irrelevant.

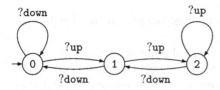

Fig. 1.13. The cabin

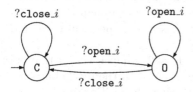

Fig. 1.14. The ith door

The controller issues instructions (the messages) to the doors and the cabin (see figure 1.15), and a more complete model would show how the controller itself reacts to requests from elevator users. The states $on i$ (respectively $free i$) correspond to the situations in which the elevator is on the ith floor with the door closed (respectively with the door open). Two additional states allow linking floor 0 to floor 2 "directly", that is, without stopping on floor 1.

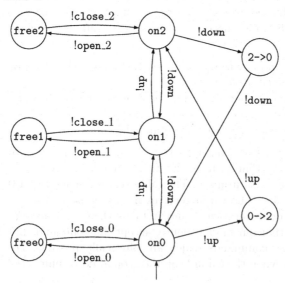

Fig. 1.15. The controller

Finally, there remains to specify the elementary propositions which hold in each state of each of the five automata. As it is often the case, we associate with each state a single elementary property, corresponding simply to the state name.

The automaton modeling the elevator is then obtained as the synchronized product of these five automata. A state of the resulting automaton will thus have five components corresponding, in that order, for example, to the state of (the automaton modeling) door 0, door 1, door 2, the cabin, and the controller. The synchronization constraints reduce to the simultaneous execution of the message emissions/receptions, formally expressed as:

$$
\begin{aligned}
\text{Sync} = \{ & (\text{?open\_1}, -, -, -, \text{!open\_1}), \ (\text{?close\_1}, -, -, -, \text{!close\_1}), \\
& (-, \text{?open\_2}, -, -, \text{!open\_2}), \ (-, \text{?close\_2}, -, -, \text{!close\_2}), \\
& (-, -, \text{?open\_3}, -, \text{!open\_3}), \ (-, -, \text{?close\_3}, -, \text{!close\_3}), \\
& (-, -, -, \text{?down}, \text{!down}), \ (-, -, -, \text{?up}, \text{!up}) \ \}.
\end{aligned}
$$

Before declaring this elevator operational, we would like to check a number of properties, for example that "the door on a given floor cannot open while the cabin is on a different floor" (P1), and that "the cabin cannot move while one of the doors is open" (P2).

For door 1, the property (P1) above translates into the fact that any state having 0 as first component necessarily has 0 as fourth component. In other words we must prove that no reachable state exists in which the first component is 0 and the fourth 1 or 2. Note that these are indeed properties expressible using the atomic propositions. The same reasoning applies to the other doors.

Expressing property (P2) is slightly more delicate. We must prove that in any execution, a state in which one of the first three components is 0 cannot be followed immediately by a state in which the fourth component has changed.

A model checker has the ability to build the synchronized product of our five automata and to check automatically whether the above properties hold. A worried reader, keen on using this elevator, can bypass the model checker, constructing the synchronized product and attempting to verify the above properties "by hand".

Asynchronous messages. There exists another way to exchange messages: asynchronous communication. We speak of *asynchronous communication* when messages are not received instantly. In general, it is assumed that messages emitted but not yet received remain somewhere within one or more *communication channels*, occasionally called *buffers*, where they are most often processed in FIFO order (*first in, first out*): messages are forwarded in the order in which they were emitted.

This model is well suited, for instance, for describing communication protocols, whereas synchronous communication is rather well suited for describing control/command systems.

Note that communication by channels can be understood directly in terms of synchronous communication. It suffices to incorporate an automaton (or a variable) representing the behavior of the channels. An emission operation from $\mathcal{A}$ to $\mathcal{A}'$ then becomes a synchronous exchange between $\mathcal{A}$ and the channel, later followed by a synchronous exchange between the channel and $\mathcal{A}'$.

If the communication channel is unbounded (it may contain an arbitrary number of messages awaiting reception) then the reachability graph is infinite. If the channels are bounded, the reachability graph potentially has exponential size (in terms of the size of the initial automaton).

1.7 Synchronization by Shared Variables

Another way to have components of a system communicate with each other is to let them share a certain number of variables. Even if, from a theoretical point of view, it is possible to present the shared variables using a synchronized product, their practical interest is such that we prefer to introduce them explicitly. We saw earlier how variables could be "added" to automata. It then is natural to allow one (or several) variable(s) to be shared by several automata.

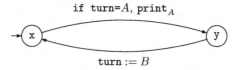

Fig. 1.16. The user A

Consider once again the case of the two users A et B who share a printer. Their unhappy experience with the unfair printer manager from section 1.3 triggered their decision to share a variable **turn** keeping track of who has the right to print.

User A is thus modeled by the automaton on figure 1.16. The automaton describing the behavior of user B is of course symmetrical (see figure 1.17).

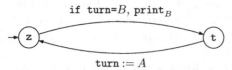

Fig. 1.17. The user B

The global automaton describing the system including both users A and B is built from these two automata and from the value of the shared variable turn. If the initial value of turn is A, the initial state of the global automaton will be (x, z, A). From this state, the only possible transition leads to (y, z, A), from which only (x, z, B), then (x, t, B) and finally (x, z, A), can be reached. We obtain a global automaton as depicted on figure 1.18.

Note that the transition guards have disappeared since we have considered only the transitions consistent with the value of the shared variable turn.

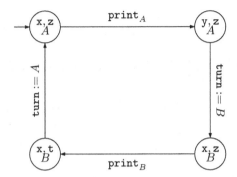

Fig. 1.18. A and B resolve conflicts on their own

A formal definition of the global automaton with shared variable synchronization can of course be given. We will not spell out this definition here, since it amounts to combining in a natural way the synchronized product and the unfolding of automata with variables, notions both already defined. We will be content with having illustrated the shared variable construction on the example of the printer users.

Obviously, the simplistic protocol implemented by the two users guarantees that no state of the form $(y, t, -)$ is reachable. The users are assured that they will never be printing simultaneously. But their protocol forbids either user from printing twice in a row!

We conclude this first chapter with a more significant example of a mutual exclusion protocol. We still strive to equip our two users of a shared printer with an adequate printer management policy. We present a simplified version of an algorithm due to Peterson [Pet81].

The two users now decide to share 3 variables:

- a variable r_A (r for "request") which the user A sets to true when he wishes to print. Initially r_A is false;
- similarly, r_B plays the corresponding role for user B;
- and again the turn variable, to settle conflicts.

The automaton modeling the behavior of user A is shown on figure 1.19 (the automaton modeling B is symmetrical, simply exchanging the roles of

A and B). As in the elevator example, we associate with each state a unique elementary proposition corresponding to its name. The property "being in state 4" corresponds to the printing of a document by the corresponding user.

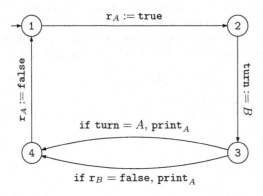

Fig. 1.19. Peterson's user A

The automaton modeling the algorithm is thus built from these two automata and from the three shared variables r_A, r_B and turn. A state is then a tuple consisting of, in that order, the state of the automaton for A, the state of the automaton for B, the value of r_A, the value of r_B and that of turn. This automaton thus has $4 \times 4 \times 2 \times 2 \times 2 = 128$ states. In fact, the number of reachable states is only 21. In particular, we can show (or ask a model checker to show) that no state of the form $(4, 4, -, -, -)$ is reachable, guaranteeing in this way that the two users cannot be printing simultaneously.

Actually, the algorithm modeled by our automaton has all the properties we sought. It ensures in particular that any print request is ultimately fulfilled. To prove such a property, we must first be able to express it in terms of the elementary propositions. This is precisely the goal of the various logics we are about to define.

2. Temporal Logic

Motivation. Let us return to the elevator example. Suppose that the requirements of the elevator includes the following properties:

- any elevator request must ultimately be satisfied;
- the elevator never traverses a floor for which a request is pending without satisfying this request.

These properties concern the *dynamic behavior* of the system. They could be formalized using notation of the kind "the position at time t", somewhat resembling the notation used in classical mechanics (the famed $z(t) = -\frac{1}{2}gt^2$ which temporarily describes a free-falling elevator) or in kinematics (a more descriptive viewpoint, in which the causes of the motion are not considered). Writing for example $H(t)$ for the cabin position at time t, and denoting by $app(n, t)$ a pending request for floor n at time t, and by $serv(n, t)$ the servicing of floor n (at time t), we could translate our two properties into the form

$$\forall t, \forall n \Big(app(n, t) \Rightarrow \exists t' > t : serv(n, t') \Big)$$

$$\forall t, \forall t' > t, \forall n \left[\begin{array}{l} \Big(app(n, t) \ \wedge \ H(t') \neq n \ \wedge \ \exists t_{\text{trav}} : \\ \quad t \leq t_{\text{trav}} \leq t' \wedge H(t_{\text{trav}}) = n \Big) \\ \Rightarrow \Big(\exists t_{\text{serv}} : t \leq t_{\text{serv}} \leq t' \wedge serv(n, t_{\text{serv}}) \Big) \end{array} \right]$$

For theoreticians, the above formulas belong to the realm of *first-order logic*. These formulas eliminate the ambiguity inherent to expressing properties in English (we assume of course that H, app, etc. are defined as well). For example, the "must ultimately be" is rendered by a $\exists t' > t$, which imposes no bound on t' (other than forbidding the equality $t' = t!$). In the same way, we have not imposed that the date t_{serv} of servicing be equal to the date t_{trav} of a floor traversing: the former is the responsibility of the implementation, and the existence of the latter is a hypothesis on the behavior.

The heavy notation used above is quite cumbersome, a blatant disadvantage. Temporal logic is a different formalism, better suited to our situation.

Temporal logic is a form of logic specifically tailored for statements and reasoning which involve the notion of order in time. A. Pnueli first suggested using it, in 1977, for the formal specification of behavioral properties of systems [Pnu77]. Compared with the mathematical formulas written above, temporal logic notation is clearer and simpler. For example, the t parameter completely disappears. Temporal logic also offers concepts immediately ready for use. Its operators mimic linguistic constructions (the adverbs "always", "until", the tenses of verbs, etc.) with the result that natural language statements and their temporal logic formalization are fairly close. Finally, temporal logic comes with a *formal semantics*, an indispensable specification language tool. .

Chapter layout. In this chapter, we will first describe the formal language of temporal logic. Then we will rigorously define its semantics. It will then be possible to appreciate, via examples, how concrete properties are expressed. We have had to choose a specific formalism out of several possible variants: for reasons of generality, we have opted for the logic known as CTL* (for *Computation Tree Logic*) introduced by Emerson and Halpern [EH86].

Of course, some experience is required to write temporal logic statements, and more experience is even needed to read statements written by others. This is one of the obstacles to the more widespread usage of model checking techniques.

This chapter will probably be hard reading for anyone with no CTL* experience, being too short to claim to cater for newcomers. Our hope is that the second part of the book will more than compensate. The second part explores in detail the different types of properties and in particular the way in which these match the different types of temporal formulas. The many examples, often viewed from a variety of angles, will undoubtedly render natural and familiar in the end what may have sounded at first like an esoteric language reserved for the initiated.

2.1 The Language of Temporal Logic

The logic CTL*, like the other temporal logics used by model checking tools, serves to formally state properties concerned with the executions of a system.

1. As we have seen in chapter 1, an execution is a sequence of states. Temporal logic uses *atomic propositions* to make statements about the states. These propositions are elementary statements which, in a given state, have a well-defined truth value. For example, we will consider that "nice_weather", "open", "in_phase_1", "x+2 = y" are propositions. Recall that these propositions are assembled into a set denoted $Prop = \{P_1, P_2, \ldots\}$ and that a proposition P is (defined as) true in a state q if and only if $P \in l(q)$.

Figure 2.1 depicts an automaton $\mathcal{A}$, the way in which its states are labelled by propositions from $Prop$, and a few of the automaton executions.

2. The classical *boolean combinators* are a necessary staple. These are the constants **true** and **false**, the negation $\neg$, and the boolean connectives $\land$

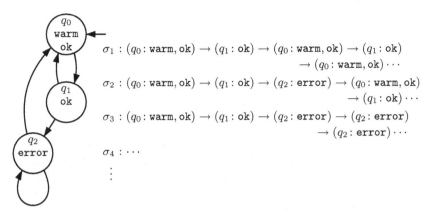

$$\sigma_1 : (q_0 : \text{warm}, \text{ok}) \rightarrow (q_1 : \text{ok}) \rightarrow (q_0 : \text{warm}, \text{ok}) \rightarrow (q_1 : \text{ok})$$
$$\rightarrow (q_0 : \text{warm}, \text{ok}) \cdots$$
$$\sigma_2 : (q_0 : \text{warm}, \text{ok}) \rightarrow (q_1 : \text{ok}) \rightarrow (q_2 : \text{error}) \rightarrow (q_0 : \text{warm}, \text{ok})$$
$$\rightarrow (q_1 : \text{ok}) \cdots$$
$$\sigma_3 : (q_0 : \text{warm}, \text{ok}) \rightarrow (q_1 : \text{ok}) \rightarrow (q_2 : \text{error}) \rightarrow (q_2 : \text{error})$$
$$\rightarrow (q_2 : \text{error}) \cdots$$
$$\sigma_4 : \cdots$$

Fig. 2.1. Atomic propositions on an automaton and its executions

(conjunction, "and"), ∨ (disjunction, "or"), ⇒ (logical implication [1]) and ⇔ (double implication, "if and only if"). These combinators allow constructing complex statements relating various simpler sub-formulas.

We speak of a *propositional formula* when referring to a mixture of propositions and boolean connectives. For example, $\text{error} \Rightarrow \neg\text{warm}$, which reads "if error then not warm", is a true propositional formula in all states of the example on figure 2.1. Note that we can tell from figure 2.1 that $\neg\text{warm}$ holds in state q_2 because $\text{warm} \notin l(q_2)$.

3. The *temporal combinators* allow one to speak about the sequencing of the states along an execution, rather than about the mere states taken individually.

The simplest combinators are X, F and G.

Whereas P states a property of the current state, XP states that the *next state* (X for "next") satisfies P. For example, $P \vee XP$ states that P is satisfied in the current state (now) or in the next state (or in both). In the example on figure 2.1, each of the three executions σ_1, σ_2 and σ_3 satisfies $XX \text{ error} \vee XXX \text{ ok}$.

FP announces that *a future state* (F for "future") satisfies P without specifying which state, and GP that *all the future states* satisfy P. These two combinators can be read informally as P *will hold some day* (at least once) and P *will always be*. We will write for example:

$$\text{alert} \Rightarrow F\,\text{halt}$$

---

[1] The logical implication sometimes leads to misunderstandings. These can be avoided by getting into the habit of reading $P \Rightarrow Q$ as "if P then Q" rather than "P implies Q". "P implies Q" suggests a causal relationship between P and Q. "If P then Q" merely bears witness to the fact that P and $\neg Q$ cannot both be true. The reader is invited to read $(1 = 2) \Rightarrow \text{Santa\_Claus\_exists}$ both ways and taste the differences.

to mean that *if* we (currently) are in a state of alert, *then* we will (*later*) be in a halt state. If we wish to declare that this property is always true, that is, that *at any time* a state of alert will necessarily be followed by a halt state *later*, we will write:

G(alert $\Rightarrow$ F halt).

In the example on figure 2.1, each occurrence of a warm state will necessarily be followed, later, by a non-warm state. Hence G(warm $\Rightarrow$ F¬warm) is true of all the executions of $\mathcal{A}$. We can even strengthen the statement and say that all the executions of $\mathcal{A}$ satisfy G(warm $\Rightarrow$ X¬warm), that is, that *it is always true that when the temperature is warm in the current state, then in the next state the temperature will not be warm.*

G is the *dual* of F: whatever the formula ϕ may be, if ϕ is always satisfied, then it is not true that ¬ϕ will some day be satisfied. Hence Gϕ and ¬F¬ϕ are equivalent [2], which we write G$\phi \equiv$ ¬F¬ϕ.

4. It is the ability to *arbitrarily nest* the various temporal combinators which gives temporal logic its power and its strength: the example G(alert $\Rightarrow$ F halt) has an F in the scope of the G. Starting from simpler formulas, temporal combinators produce new formulas whose meaning derives from the meaning of its components (called *sub-formulas*).

The nesting of F and G is very often used to express repetition properties. Thus GFϕ which, literally, must be read as *always there will some day be a state such that* ϕ, expresses that ϕ is satisfied infinitely often along the execution considered. This construct is so ubiquitous that we use the abbreviation $\overset{\infty}{F}$ (read "infinitely often") for GF. The dual is $\overset{\infty}{G}$, abbreviation of FG, read as "all the time from a certain time onwards", or "at each time instant, possibly excluding a finite number of instants".

Consider an execution from figure 2.1. Two cases are possible: either it visits the state warm infinitely often, or it ultimately remains in state error forever. Consequently, all the executions satisfy the formula $\overset{\infty}{F}$ warm $\vee$ $\overset{\infty}{G}$ error.

5. The U combinator (for *until*, not to be confused with the set union symbol!) is richer and more complicated. $\phi_1 U \phi_2$ states that ϕ_1 is verified *until* ϕ_2 is verified. More precisely: ϕ_2 will be verified some day, and ϕ_1 will hold in the meantime. The example G(alert $\Rightarrow$ F halt) can be completed with the statement that "starting from a state of alert, the alarm remains activated until the halt state is eventually and inexorably reached":

G(alert $\Rightarrow$ (alarm U halt)).

The F combinator is a special case of U in that Fϕ and true Uϕ are equivalent.

---

[2] This is equivalence in the strong sense of logic. Two formulas are *equivalent* if and only if they carry the same meaning, thus hold in the same models, and can replace each other's occurrence as sub-formulas of a larger formula.

There exists a "weak *until*", denoted W. The statement $\phi_1 W \phi_2$ still expresses "ϕ_1 until ϕ_2", but without the inexorable occurrence of ϕ_2 (and if ϕ_2 never occurs, then ϕ_1 remains true until the end). This can also be read as "ϕ_1 while not ϕ_2". Note that W is expressible in terms of U:

$$\phi_1 W \phi_2 \;\equiv\; (\phi_1 U \phi_2) \vee G \phi_1.$$

In the example on figure 2.1, all the executions originating in state q_0 satisfy ok W error but there exists a (unique) execution from state q_0 which does not satisfy ok U error.

6. The logic introduced so far can only state properties of one execution. There remains to express the tree aspect of the behavior (many futures are possible starting from a given state). Special purpose quantifiers, A and E, allow one to quantify over the set of executions. These are also called *path quantifiers*.

The formula $A\phi$ states that *all the executions* out of the current state satisfy property ϕ, whereas $E\phi$ states that from the current state, *there exists an execution* satisfying ϕ.

One must not confuse A and G: $A\phi$ states that all the executions currently possible satisfy ϕ, and $G\phi$ states that ϕ holds at every time step of the one execution being considered. More generally, A and E quantify over paths, F and G quantify over positions along a given path.

The A and E combinators on the one hand, G and F on the other, are often used in pairs. For example, EFP states that it is possible (by following a suitable execution) to have P some day. AFP states that we will necessarily have P some day (regardless of the chosen execution). Herein lies the difference between the possible and the unavoidable. AGP states that P is always true [3] whereas EGP states that *there exists* an execution along which P always holds. Figure 2.2 illustrates the four possible combinations of E or A with F or G.

Let us return to the example on figure 2.1. We note that all the executions out of q_0 end up traversing q_1. Now, from q_1 it is possible in one step to reach a state satisfying error. Hence any execution out of q_0 satisfies F EX error. Note that using the E quantifier is crucial, and that there exists an execution which does not satisfy F X error.

"Branching time logics" refer to logics which have this capability to freely quantify over the paths that are possible.

The role played by the quantifiers stands out clearly in the difference between the formulas $AGFP$ and $AGEFP$. The former states that along every execution (A), at every time instant (G), we will necessarily encounter later (F) a state satisfying P. Hence P will necessarily be satisfied infinitely often regardless of the course of action actually taken by the system, as is clearly

---

[3] We also say that P is an *invariant*. Invariants are properties that are true continuously. We will come across these again in chapter 7 dealing with safety properties.

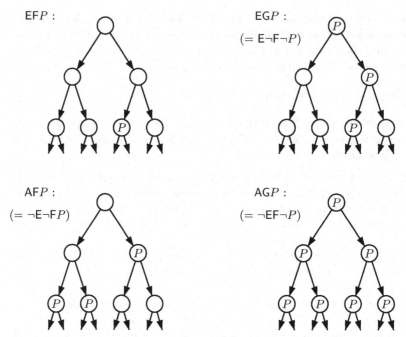

Fig. 2.2. Four ways of combining E and F

stated by the equivalent expression $A \overset{\infty}{F} P$. The second formula, $AG\,EFP$, states that at any instant of any execution it would be possible to reach P, otherwise stated as P is always potentially reachable. $AG\,EFP$ can be verified even if there exists an execution in which P is never realized. Along every execution, the second quantifier (E) allows expressing the fact that alternative executions exist which would carry on the system behavior in different ways.

In CTL*, A and E are duals of one another, as is usual for universal and existential quantifiers. Indeed, if $A\phi$ is not verified, then there exists an execution which does not satisfy ϕ, and hence satisfies $\neg\phi$. Thus $A\phi$ and $\neg E\neg\phi$ are equivalent.

2.2 The Formal Syntax of Temporal Logic

The concepts presented and illustrated above naturally lead to the following formal grammar for CTL*:

$$\phi, \psi \; ::= \; P_1 \mid P_2 \mid \dots \qquad \text{(atomic proposition)}$$
$$\mid \neg\phi \mid \phi \wedge \psi \mid \phi \Rightarrow \psi \mid \dots \quad \text{(boolean combinators)}$$
$$\mid X\phi \mid F\phi \mid G\phi \mid \phi U\psi \mid \dots \quad \text{(temporal combinators)}$$
$$\mid E\phi \mid A\phi \qquad \text{(path quantifiers).}$$

This is an abstract grammar. In practice, each tool dealing with temporal formulas will allow parentheses, and will have its own operator priority conventions. As well, each tool will have its specific set of atomic propositions and combinators. Most importantly, as a rule of thumb the scope of a model checker will be restricted to a fragment of CTL*, most often CTL or PLTL (see section 2.4).

2.3 The Semantics of Temporal Logic

Which models. The models of temporal logic are called *Kripke structures*. For us, this is just another name for automata, with a subtle word of caution: the propositions which label the states of an automaton play a fundamental role in a *state-based* [4] logic such as CTL*, and the actions which label the automaton transitions have less importance.

The transition labels played a fundamental role in chapter 1 where they allowed us to synchronize several sub-systems. In book chapters such as this chapter 2, wholly concerned with temporal logic, we will neglect these transition labels completely and we will consider automata $\mathcal{A} = \langle Q, T, q_0, l \rangle$ with $T \subseteq Q \times Q$. On the other hand we will make heavy use here of the labelling l which associates with each state $q \in Q$ the set $l(q)$ of atomic propositions verified by q. Recall that this labelling is an essential part of the modeling afforded by an automaton: the structure of the automaton and the propositions which label its states are designed simultaneously, as part of one and the same modeling process.

Satisfaction. We will now formally define the notion of a "formula satisfied in a given situation". The discussion and the examples of the preceding section show that a formula of CTL* refers to a given instant of an execution of a given automaton.

We will write $\mathcal{A}, \sigma, i \models \phi$ and we will read "at time i of the execution σ, ϕ is true", where σ is an execution of $\mathcal{A}$ which we do not require to start at the initial state. The *context* $\mathcal{A}$ is very often left implicit and is omitted from our writing. We write $\sigma, i \not\models \phi$ to state that ϕ *is not satisfied* at time i of σ.

Defining $\sigma, i \models \phi$ is done by induction on the structure of ϕ. That is, the truth value of a composite formula is given as a function of the truth values of its sub-formulas.

Figure 2.3 thus lists nine definition clauses corresponding to nine different ways to construct a temporal formula from sub-formulas. (Recall that $\sigma(i)$ is the i-th state of σ and that $|\sigma|$ is the length of σ.) The clauses for the derived operators ($\Rightarrow$, $\vee$, $\overset{\infty}{F}$, W, etc.) can be deduced and are not explicitly mentioned,

---

[4] Of course there exist so-called *action-based* CTL* variants, tailored for automata in which the transition labels are the most relevant. The two viewpoints are very similar [DV90] and we adopt one or the other according to the models with which we work.

$$
\begin{array}{ll}
\sigma, i \models P & \text{iff } P \in l(\sigma(i)), \\
\sigma, i \models \neg\phi & \text{iff it is not true that } \sigma, i \models \phi, \\
\sigma, i \models \phi \wedge \psi & \text{iff } \sigma, i \models \phi \text{ and } \sigma, i \models \psi, \\
\\
\sigma, i \models \mathsf{X}\phi & \text{iff } i < |\sigma| \text{ and } \sigma, i+1 \models \phi, \\
\sigma, i \models \mathsf{F}\phi & \text{iff there exists } j \text{ such that } i \leq j \leq |\sigma| \text{ and } \sigma, j \models \phi, \\
\sigma, i \models \mathsf{G}\phi & \text{iff for all } j \text{ such that } i \leq j \leq |\sigma|, \text{ we have } \sigma, j \models \phi, \\
\\
\sigma, i \models \phi \mathsf{U}\psi & \text{iff there exists } j, i \leq j \leq |\sigma| \text{ such that } \sigma, j \models \psi, \text{ and} \\
& \quad \text{for all } k \text{ such that } i \leq k < j, \text{ we have } \sigma, k \models \phi, \\
\\
\sigma, i \models \mathsf{E}\phi & \text{iff there exists a } \sigma' \text{ such that } \sigma(0)\ldots\sigma(i) = \sigma'(0)\ldots\sigma'(i) \text{ and} \\
& \quad \sigma', i \models \phi, \\
\sigma, i \models \mathsf{A}\phi & \text{iff for all } \sigma' \text{ such that } \sigma(0)\ldots\sigma(i) = \sigma'(0)\ldots\sigma'(i), \text{ we have} \\
& \quad \sigma', i \models \phi.
\end{array}
$$

Fig. 2.3. Semantics of CTL*

some of the clauses mentioned (those for F, G and A) are redundant and could be deduced from the others.

We are ready to introduce a derived notion, "the automaton $\mathcal{A}$ satisfies ϕ", denoted $\mathcal{A} \models \phi$, and defined by:

$$
\mathcal{A} \models \phi \text{ iff } \sigma, 0 \models \phi \text{ for every execution } \sigma \text{ of } \mathcal{A}. \tag{D1}
$$

This notion comes in very handy when we discuss the correctness of a model. But it is not elementary in that it treats as a group the correctness of all the executions (out of q_0) of a model. Thus, $\mathcal{A} \not\models \phi$ does not necessarily imply $\mathcal{A} \models \neg\phi$ (whereas $\sigma, i \not\models \phi$ is equivalent to $\sigma, i \models \neg\phi$).

The nature of time. We recognize in the definitions on figure 2.3 the cumbersome nature of the first-order formulas encountered on page 27. The "there exists j such that $i \leq j \leq |\sigma|\ldots$" pertaining to the F clause is reminiscent of $\exists t' \geq t$. Indeed, in a statement of the form $\sigma, i \models \phi$, the parameter i records the passage of time along σ. Nonetheless, an important difference between the two frameworks exists. The semantics of CTL* touch on the nature of time: the instants are the points along the executions. The first-order formulas leave the nature of time implicit. When we write $\exists t' > t$, where is t'? Later in the same execution or later in a different execution? And to begin with, what is t? If we should want to formalize requirements with the use of first-order formulas, it would be necessary to address all these questions, that is, to choose a model of time.

In CTL*, time is *discrete*, as opposed to *continuous* or *dense*. In CTL* nothing exists between i and $i+1$. Temporal logic makes the time parameter implicit: any statement implicitly refers to a current time step. And its choice of combinators fixes once and for all the constructs that can be used. Properties more easily expressed in first-order logic do exist but they are rare. One could say that temporal logic, as opposed to first-order logic, is like a high level language which would compile in machine language.

2.4 PLTL and CTL: Two Temporal Logics

PLTL (*Propositional Linear Temporal Logic*) and CTL (*Computation Tree Logic*) are the two most commonly used temporal logics in model checking tools. Their origins differ (PLTL reaches back to [Pnu81] and CTL to [CE81, EH82]) but each may be viewed as a fragment of CTL*.

– PLTL is the fragment obtained from CTL* by withholding the A and E quantifiers. Thus, a formula PLTL ϕ, in the context of a given execution, cannot examine alternative executions which split off from this one at each time step where a nondeterministic choice is possible. PLTL only deals with the set of executions and not with the way in which these are organized into a tree. We then speak of *path formulas* and sometimes use the somewhat barbaric terminology "linear time logic" for this kind of formalism.

For example, PLTL cannot express that at some instants along an execution it would be possible to extend the execution in this or that way. Characteristically, the property "*P* is always potentially reachable", which we have expressed earlier as AG EFP, cannot be expressed in PLTL.

Figure 2.4 depicts two automata $\mathcal{A}_1$ and $\mathcal{A}_2$ which PLTL cannot tell apart.

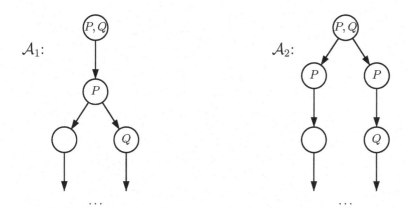

Fig. 2.4. Two automata, indistinguishable for PLTL

Seen from PLTL, these two automata correspond to one and the same set of paths, of the form:

seen from execution 1: $\{P,Q\} . \{P\} . \{\_\} \ldots$
seen from execution 2: $\{P,Q\} . \{P\} . \{Q\} \ldots$

and if a PLTL formula ϕ holds of one, it holds of the other. Note that there exists a CTL formula (see below) true of $\mathcal{A}_1$ and false of $\mathcal{A}_2$.

– CTL is the fragment obtained from CTL* by requiring that each use of a temporal combinator (X, F, U, etc.) be under the immediate scope of a A or E quantifier. The combinators available to CTL can thus be taken to be EX, AX, E_U_, A_U_ and their derivatives: EF, etc. For example, the four combinators on figure 2.2 are CTL constructs.

The criterion is syntactic. Hence $\mathsf{E}P\mathsf{U}\mathsf{A}(P_2\mathsf{U}P_3)$ and $\mathsf{E}P\mathsf{U}\mathsf{E}(P_2\mathsf{U}P_3)$ are CTL formulas but $\mathsf{E}P\mathsf{U}(P_2\mathsf{U}P_3)$ is not because the U in $P_2\mathsf{U}P_3$ is not in the immediate scope of a quantifier. And yet, $\mathsf{E}P\mathsf{U}(P_2\mathsf{U}P_3)$ is equivalent to $\mathsf{E}P\mathsf{U}\mathsf{E}(P_2\mathsf{U}P_3)$ which is a CTL formula indeed. (Note that $\mathsf{E}\overset{\infty}{\mathsf{F}}P$ is not a CTL formula because $\overset{\infty}{\mathsf{F}}$ is an abbreviation for GF.)

The need to always quantify over the possible futures noticeably limits the expressivity of CTL. It is impossible to nest several temporal combinators while continuously referring to "one execution". A consequence is that CTL formulas are *state formulas* [5]. Their truth only depends on the current state (and the automata regions made reachable by it), it does not depend on a current execution. This limitation carries its benefits, as will be seen in chapter 3.

When considering state formulas, it is customary to write $q \models \phi$ to mean that ϕ is satisfied "in state q".

Returning to the example on figure 2.4, it is possible in CTL to distinguish $\mathcal{A}_1$ from $\mathcal{A}_2$ by expressing the fact that the choice between $Q \wedge \neg P$ on the one hand, and $\neg Q \wedge \neg P$ on the other, remains open longer in $\mathcal{A}_1$ than in $\mathcal{A}_2$, since $\mathcal{A}_1, q_0 \models \mathsf{AX}(\mathsf{EX}Q \wedge \mathsf{EX}\neg Q)$ whereas $\mathcal{A}_2, q_0' \not\models \mathsf{AX}(\mathsf{EX}Q \wedge \mathsf{EX}\neg Q)$.

In the same spirit, CTL allows us to express the potential reachability by AG EFP but does not allow us to express very rich properties along the paths. For example, the existence of a path satisfying P infinitely often ($\mathsf{E}\overset{\infty}{\mathsf{F}}P$ in CTL*) simply cannot be expressed in CTL. Often, we settle for an approximation such as $\neg\mathsf{AF}\neg\mathsf{EF}P$ which states that "it is not true that we will necessarily reach a state some day from which P can never happen again". This latter property is strictly weaker than $\mathsf{E}\overset{\infty}{\mathsf{F}}P$: imagine a system in which a self-loop allows us to remain in the initial state for as long as we wish, before possibly choosing a computation along which P is possible only once. Then $\mathsf{E}\overset{\infty}{\mathsf{F}}P$ is not verified. However, by remaining forever in the initial state, we always verify EFP. The system thus satisfies $\neg\mathsf{AF}\neg\mathsf{EF}P$ but not $\mathsf{E}\overset{\infty}{\mathsf{F}}P$.

---

[5] Formally, we will say that a formula ϕ is a *state formula* if $\sigma, i \models \phi$ only depends on the current state $\sigma(i)$, that is if for all executions σ and σ' we have as a consequence of $\sigma(i) = \sigma'(j)$ that $(\sigma, i \models \phi$ iff $\sigma', j \models \phi)$.

Which to choose, PLTL *or* CTL. In theory, CTL and PLTL each have their strengths and weaknesses when it comes to expressivity. This is in fact what led to the definition of CTL*, proposed after CTL and PLTL.

In practice, we attempt to describe the behavior expected of a system, the shortcomings of CTL are more embarrassing than those of PLTL. Most weaknesses of CTL disappear with the use of FCTL (*F* for "fair"), an extension of CTL which allows us to express fairness properties such as $\mathsf{E}(\overset{\approx}{\mathsf{F}} P \wedge \overset{\approx}{\mathsf{F}} Q)$ [EH86, EL87].

However, the disadvantages of CTL are compensated by the fact that model checking in CTL is much more efficient than model checking in PLTL. (FCTL essentially allows for model checking in polynomial time [EL87].)

The right choice is thus a compromise which depends on several factors. If our goal is to state some properties, then we will opt for PLTL (or even for CTL* which however has the disadvantage of being both less popular and technically more complicated than PLTL). If we aim for the exhaustive verification of a system, then a specification in CTL is more likely to avoid the combinatorial explosion pitfall. If we wish to perform verification on-the-fly in order to detect possible errors, but we do not aim for exhaustivity, then PLTL is a good choice. If we are required to use this or that specific tool, this tool will impose its temporal logic language and no choice will be offered. The main tools use either CTL (for example SMV) or PLTL (for example SPIN) and we can lament the fact that the usage of FCTL is not more widespread (SMV allows writing fairness constraints in the model definition, not in the temporal formulas).

2.5 The Expressivity of CTL*

After this quick survey, the reader must certainly wonder whether CTL* allows to express the properties of interest in practice?

Note first that no logic can express anything not taken into account by the modeling decisions made. The automata encountered in chapter 1 encompass no *stochastic* notion such as for example the probability of choosing one transition rather than another. Also, our automata never suffer from *failures*, and their transitions have no *duration*. Thus, it would make no sense to consider stochastic or timing properties of these automata: other models are required, for example timed automata, which will be described in chapter 5.

When the properties concern the execution tree of our automata, CTL* is rather expressive enough. Theoreticians have obtained many theorems uncovering the fundamental aspects of this question. We mention two which seem of particular interest:

- any property of the form "as seen from the outside world, the automaton $\mathcal{A}$ being studied behaves like the reference automaton $\mathcal{B}$" can be expressed in CTL. Concretely, for any $\mathcal{B}$, a CTL formula $\phi_{\mathcal{B}}$ can be produced to mean "to be like $\mathcal{B}$", that is, such that for every $\mathcal{A}$, $\mathcal{A} \models \phi_{\mathcal{B}}$ if and only if $\mathcal{A}$ and $\mathcal{B}$ are indistinguishable as seen from the outside [BCG88];

- the CTL* combinators are sufficiently expressive. A theorem due to Kamp [Kam68, GPSS80] shows that any new temporal combinator whose semantics can be expressed as a clause similar [6] to the clauses of figure 2.3 can be defined as an expression based on X and U. For example, a Z combinator defined by "$\sigma \models \phi Z \psi$ if and only if between each pair of states satisfying ϕ we can find a state (strictly in between) satisfying ψ" can be expressed using U and X:

$$\phi Z \psi \;\equiv\; G\Big(\phi \Rightarrow X\big(\neg\phi W(\psi \wedge \neg\phi)\big)\Big).$$

From a practical point of view, CTL* is almost always sufficient. It rarely happens that an interesting property cannot be expressed. In fact, we are often faced rather with the problem that a property is expressible, but not naturally, as we will see in the second part of this book.

---

[6] Formally, any first-order formula having $\leq$ as the only predicate is allowed.

3. Model Checking

In this chapter we describe the principles underlying the *algorithms* used for model checking, that is, the algorithms which can find out whether a given automaton satisfies a given temporal formula.

We consider the model checking problem for the logic CTL and that for PLTL separately. These two questions call for somewhat different answers and the corresponding algorithms were developed independently.

3.1 Model Checking CTL

The model checking algorithm for CTLwas initially developed by Queille, Sifakis, Clarke, Emerson and Sistla [QS82, CES86] and was later improved (see for example [CGL94a]).

This fundamental algorithm plays a very important role in the area of verification. This is due in part to the fact that the algorithm runs in time linear in each of its components (the automaton on the one hand, and the CTL formula on the other). The algorithm relies on the fact that CTL can only express state formulas (see section 2.4). Indeed, this characteristic of CTL allows us to reason in terms of which states satisfy which formulas, rather than considering the executions which are the true objects of our interest.

Basic principle. The fundamental component of the model checking algorithm for CTL is a procedure `marking` which operates on an automaton $\mathcal{A}$ and which, starting from a CTL formula ϕ, will mark, for each state q of the automaton and for each sub-formula ψ of ϕ, whether ψ is satisfied in state q. In the end, for each state and each sub-formula, `q.psi` holds the value `true` if $q \models \psi$, `false` otherwise.

We use the term "marking" to mean that the value of `q.psi` is computed then memorized. Memorizing is important because the marking of `q.phi` uses the values of `q'.psi` for sub-formulas `psi` of `phi` and for states `q'` reachable from `q`. When the marking for `phi` is completed, it is easy to say whether $\mathcal{A} \models \phi$ by looking up the value of `q0.phi` for the initial state q_0 of $\mathcal{A}$. Here is the crux of the algorithm:

```
procedure marking(phi)

  case 1: phi = P
    for all q in Q, if P in l(q) then do q.phi := true,
                                   else do q.phi := false.

  case 2: phi = not psi
    do marking(psi);
    for all q in Q, do q.phi := not(q.psi).

  case 3: phi = psi1 /\ psi2
    do marking(psi1); marking(psi2);
    for all q in Q, do q.phi := and(q.psi1, q.psi2).

  case 4: phi = EX psi
    do marking(psi);
    for all q in Q, do q.phi := false;        /* initialisation */
    for all (q,q') in T, if q'.psi = true then do q.phi := true.

  case 5: phi = E psi1 U psi2
    do marking(psi1); marking(psi2);
    for all q in Q,
      q.phi := false; q.seenbefore := false;/* initialisation */
    L := {};                         /* L: states to be processed */
    for all q in Q, if q.psi2 = true then do L := L + { q };
    while L nonempty {
      draw q from L;                              /* must mark q */
      L := L - { q };
      q.phi := true;
      for all (q',q) in T {        /* q' is a predecessor of q */
        if q'.seenbefore = false then do {
          q'.seenbefore := true;
          if q'.psi1 = true then do L := L + { q' };
        }
      }
    }

  case 6: phi = A psi1 U psi2
  /* See further */
```

We see how simple the marking is when ϕ is an atomic proposition (case 1), a negation (case 2) or a conjunction (case 3). In each of these three cases, the marking for ϕ only requires one pass over Q – in time $O(|Q|)$ – plus the work required to mark the sub-formulas of ϕ.

When ϕ is of the form $EX\psi$ (case 4), the marking only requires a pass over T (the set of transitions of the automaton). Hence this step uses no more than time $O(|T|)$, added to the initialization and the marking time for ψ. The case $AX\psi$ was not treated: it is equivalent to $\neg EX\neg\psi$.

When ϕ is of the form $E\psi_1 U\psi_2$ (case 5), the marking of ϕ starting from the markings of ψ_1 and ψ_2 uses a standard algorithm for controlled reachability in a graph (with the proviso that the transitions are traversed backwards).

We have chosen to describe such an algorithm in detail in order to stress how this step can be implemented without visiting each transition $(q, q') \in T$ more than once, so as to perform the computation in time $O(|Q| + |T|)$.

The marking algorithm for ϕ of the form $A\psi_1 U \psi_2$ (case 6) is a bit more complicated (see below). It relies on the observation that a state q satisfies $A\psi_1 U \psi_2$ if and only if either (a) q satisfies ψ_2, or (b.1) q satisfies ψ_1, (b.2) q has at least one successor state, and (b.3) all its successors satisfy $A\psi_1 U \psi_2$. The marking algorithm will keep a counter **nb** associated with each state. Initially, **q.nb** is set to $degree(q)$, that is the number of successors of q in the graph of the automaton. Then, each time a successor of q is marked as satisfying $A\psi_1 U \psi_2$, the counter of q is decremented. When after decrementing **q.nb** reaches value 0, we know that all the successors of q satisfy $A\psi_1 U \psi_2$. If moreover q satisfies ψ_1, then we know that it satisfies ϕ.

```
case 6: phi = A psi1 U psi2
  do marking(psi1); marking(psi2);
  L := {}                        /* L: states to be processed */
  for all q in Q,
    q.nb := degree(q); q.phi := false;      /* initialisation */
  for all q in Q, if q.psi2 = true then do L := L + { q };
  while L nonempty {
    draw q from L;                          /* must mark q */
    L := L - { q };
    q.phi := true;
    for all (q',q) in T {          /* q' is a predecessor of q */
      q'.nb := q'.nb - 1;                        /* decrement */
      if (q'.nb = 0) and (q'.psi1 = true) and (q'.phi = false)
        then do L := L + { q' };
    }
  }
```

It remains to verify the correctness of this method, more complex for $A\psi_1 U \psi_2$ than for the other cases. Termination is obvious: each state can only be added once to the set L of states to be processed.

Correctness of the algorithm. To facilitate reading the code, we will prove correctness of the final marking in the case where ϕ has the form $A\psi_1 U \psi_2$ (the other cases are simpler). For this we assume (by induction) that the marking of the sub-formulas ψ_1 and ψ_2 is correct. To begin with, it is easy to see that if **q.phi** is ever set to **true** during the marking, then q satisfies ϕ. The converse is harder to see. To see it we imagine **q.phi** holding **false** at the end of the traversal. Then necessarily $q \not\models \psi_2$. If moreover $q \not\models \psi_1$, then $q \not\models \phi$ and the value of **q.phi** is correct. If $q \models \psi_1$ (and if $degree(q) \neq 0$), then necessarily **q.nb** is strictly positive at the end of the marking (else q would have been inserted into L). Hence one of the successors of q, say q_1, holds a marking **q1.phi** equal to **false**. The same reasoning applies to q_1. It does not satisfy ψ_2 and if it satisfies ψ_1 it has a successor, say q_2, which is not marked for ϕ. And so on, so that we are led to exhibit an execution out of q along which $\psi_1 U \psi_2$ is not verified. This proves that $q \not\models \phi$. Hence the marking of q is correct.

Complexity of the algorithm. The complexity analysis (including the termination proof) is simple: each step in the algorithm is associated either with the marking of a node $q \in Q$, or with the processing of a transition (q', q) of T. Hence, once the markings for ψ_1 and ψ_2 are complete, the time required to mark ϕ is in $O(|Q| + |T|)$, that is $O(|\mathcal{A}|)$.

Finally, the marking for an arbitrary formula ϕ requires a marking for the sub-formulas of ϕ followed by a step specific to ϕ, which step requires time $O(|\mathcal{A}|)$. The total time required for the complete marking is thus in $O(|\mathcal{A}| \times |\phi|)$.

Model checking "does $\mathcal{A}, q_0 \models \phi$?" for a CTL formula ϕ can be solved in time $O(|\mathcal{A}| \times |\phi|)$.

3.2 Model Checking PLTL

The principle underlying the model checking algorithm for PLTL is essentially due to Lichtenstein, Pnueli, Vardi and Wolper [LP85, VW86]. Our treatment will avoid certain details which are too technical: for these the reader will refer to the very clear [Var96].

In the case of PLTL we no longer deal with state formulas and it is no longer possible to rely on marking the automaton states. The formulas of PLTL are *path formulas* (see section 2.4) and a finite automaton will generally give rise to infinitely many different executions, themselves often infinite in length. In this context, the viewpoint adopted will be language theory.

Consider for example the following formula ϕ: $\overset{\infty}{F} P$. An execution q_0, q_1, $q_2, \ldots$ satisfying ϕ must contain infinitely many positions $q_{n_1}, q_{n_2}, \ldots$ at which P holds. Between each of these positions there can be an arbitrary (though finite) number of states satisfying $\neg P$. We will say that the execution is of the form $((\neg P)^* . P)^\omega$.

In the same spirit, an execution which does not satisfy ϕ must, from a certain position onwards, only contain states satisfying $\neg P$. Such an execution is said to be of the form $(P + \neg P)^* . (\neg P)^\omega$.

The two notations which we have just used to express the form required of an execution satisfying ϕ (respectively, not satisfying ϕ) are *ω-regular expressions* . These extend the well-known notion of a *regular expression* [1],

---

[1] Regular expressions are a notation allowing the succinct description of regular sets of words. This notation uses the symbol "+" to represent union (or the possible choice) and star "*" (as an exponent) to represent an arbitrary but finite number of repetitions. For example $(a\, b^* + c)^*$ stands for the set of all words which are an arbitrary sequence of segments of the form either c, or a followed by an arbitrary number of bs.

extension used to deal with languages of infinite words. In the ω-regular expressions we adjoin to the classical exponent "$*$" (meaning *an arbitrary but finite number of* repetitions) a new exponent "ω" meaning an *infinite number* of repetitions.

Basic principle. Model checking PLTL relies on the possibility to associate with each PLTL formula ϕ an ω-regular expression $\mathcal{E}_\phi$ describing the form imposed on an execution by its satisfaction of ϕ. The "does $\mathcal{A} \models \phi$?" question then reduces to a "are all the executions of $\mathcal{A}$ of the form described by $\mathcal{E}_\phi$?" question.

In practice, the algorithms do not reason on the regular expressions themselves but on automata [2]. A PLTL model checker will, given a formula ϕ, construct an automaton $\mathcal{B}_{\neg\phi}$ that recognizes precisely the executions which do not satisfy ϕ. (The size of this automaton is $O(2^{|\phi|})$ in the worst case). We strongly synchronize (that is, in such a way that the two automata progress simultaneously, see section 1.5) $\mathcal{A}$ and $\mathcal{B}_{\neg\phi}$ to obtain an automaton, denoted $\mathcal{A} \otimes \mathcal{B}_{\neg\phi}$, whose sole behaviors are the behaviors of $\mathcal{A}$ accepted by $\mathcal{B}_{\neg\phi}$, in other words the executions of $\mathcal{A}$ which do not satisfy ϕ.

The model checking problem "does $\mathcal{A} \models \phi$?" thus reduces to the "is the language recognized by $\mathcal{A} \otimes \mathcal{B}_{\neg\phi}$ empty?" problem.

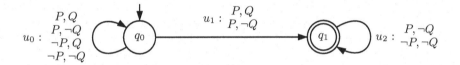

Fig. 3.1. $\mathcal{B}_{\neg\phi}$ for $\phi : \mathsf{G}(P \Rightarrow \mathsf{X}\,\mathsf{F}Q)$

A simple example. Figure 3.1 depicts an automaton $\mathcal{B}_{\neg\phi}$ for a formula ϕ stating that any occurrence of P must be followed (later) by an occurrence of Q, which is written $\mathsf{G}(P \Rightarrow \mathsf{X}\,\mathsf{F}Q)$ in PLTL. Thence, $\neg\phi$ means that there exists an occurrence of P after which we will never again encounter Q. The operation of $\mathcal{B}_{\neg\phi}$ thus becomes clear. This automaton is not deterministic. It can choose, at any time at which P is verified, to move from q_0 to q_1, guessing that Q will never hold again. If it successfully remains in q_1 indefinitely without blocking, then it will indeed observe a behavior violating ϕ. This is what we have indicated by representing q_1 by means of a double circle.

---

[2] A very tight correspondence between the two notions exists, which is the content of the fundamental theorem of Kleene and its extensions: a language is definable by a regular expression if and only if it is a language recognizable by a finite automaton.

Note here that the *transitions* of $\mathcal{B}_{\neg\phi}$ are labelled by valuations of the atomic propositions P and Q. This allows $\mathcal{B}_{\neg\phi}$ to observe the propositions appearing along an execution.

We can now verify the automaton $\mathcal{A}$ from figure 3.2.

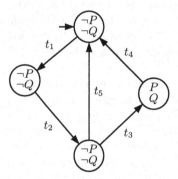

Fig. 3.2. Does the automaton $\mathcal{A}$ verify $\phi : \mathsf{G}(P \Rightarrow \mathsf{X}\,\mathsf{F}Q)$?

The automaton $\mathcal{A} \otimes \mathcal{B}_{\neg\phi}$ from figure 3.3 results from the synchronization of our two automata, modulo the fact that the propositions label the *states* of $\mathcal{A}$ and the *transitions* of $\mathcal{B}_{\neg\phi}$, which leads to an adaptation of the synchronization operation used so far. In accordance with $\mathcal{B}_{\neg\phi}$, a transition $t \otimes u_1$ is only possible if t leaves from a state satisfying P (a state q such that $l(q) = \{P,Q\}$ or $l(q) = \{P\}$), whereas a transition $t \otimes u_2$ is possible only if t leaves from a state satisfying $\neg Q$ ($l(q) = \{P\}$ or $l(q) = \{\}$). This explains why $\mathcal{A} \otimes \mathcal{B}_{\neg\phi}$ only has 10 transitions instead of the theoretical maximum of 5×3.

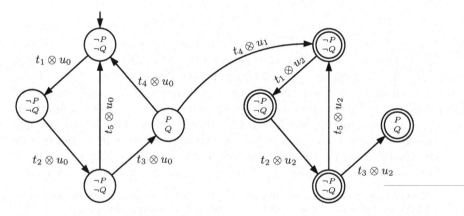

Fig. 3.3. The product $\mathcal{A} \otimes \mathcal{B}_{\neg\phi}$

We observe that there are behaviors of $\mathcal{A}$ accepted by $\mathcal{A} \otimes \mathcal{B}_{\neg\phi}$, that is, which from a certain time onwards remain in the "double-circle" states indefinitely. For this it suffices to reach the right hand part of the system and to avoid blocking. In this way, the language recognized by $\mathcal{A} \otimes \mathcal{B}_{\neg\phi}$ is nonempty and we can state that $\mathcal{A} \not\models \phi$.

The preceding example only aimed at conveying the essential features of the model checking algorithm for PLTL. We have skimmed over technical details, the hardest of which is the automatic construction of $\mathcal{B}_{\neg\phi}$ (the reader is referred to [Var96]). Note moreover that the automaton $\mathcal{B}_{\neg\phi}$ must in general be able to recognize infinite words, requiring for example *Büchi automata* [3].

Nevertheless, from the complexity viewpoint, the essential aspects of the construction are the following:

- $\mathcal{B}_{\neg\phi}$ has size $O(2^{|\phi|})$ in the worst case;
- the product $\mathcal{A} \otimes \mathcal{B}_{\neg\phi}$ has size $O(|\mathcal{A}| \times |\mathcal{B}_{\neg\phi}|)$;
- if $\mathcal{A} \otimes \mathcal{B}_{\neg\phi}$ fits in computer memory, we can determine whether it accepts a nonempty language in time $O(|\mathcal{A} \otimes \mathcal{B}_{\neg\phi}|)$.

Model checking "does $\mathcal{A}, q_0 \models \phi$?" for a PLTL formula ϕ can be done in time $O(|\mathcal{A}| \times 2^{|\phi|})$.

In a sense, we can say that the automaton $\mathcal{B}_{\neg\phi}$ *observes* the behavior of $\mathcal{A}$ when the two automata are synchronized. Indeed, it is possible to use this same principle to perform the model checking of PLTL formulas whenever a tool to synchronize automata and to decide reachability is available. This is the case for example with the UPPAAL tool (see chapter 15) which advertises no model checking algorithm for PLTL. We note then that the user usually defines an automaton observing the undesired behaviors without an intermediate temporal logic statement for the desired properties. The observer automaton (or *test automaton*) is itself the formal specification of the desired property.

In the SPIN tool (see chapter 13), the PLTL model checking explicitly constructs $\mathcal{B}_{\neg\phi}$ and this automaton is made available to the user. One can modify it, adapt it, etc. The tool also allows a user to construct the observer automaton without the need for temporal logic.

3.3 The State Explosion Problem

The main obstacle encountered by model checking algorithms is the so-called *state explosion problem*.

---

[3] A Büchi automaton is an automaton designed to recognize (or generate) infinite words. The rule followed by a Büchi automaton is not to "end in an accepting state", but rather to traverse accepting states infinitely often in the course of its computation. See [Tho90].

Indeed, the algorithms presented above rely on the explicit construction of the automaton $\mathcal{A}$ targeted for verification: $\mathcal{A}$ is subjected to traversals and markings (case of CTL), and to the synchronization with $\mathcal{B}_{\neg\phi}$ and the seeking of reachable states and loops (case of PLTL).

In practice the number of states of $\mathcal{A}$ is quickly very large. When $\mathcal{A}$ is built by synchronizing the components $\mathcal{A}_1, \ldots, \mathcal{A}_n$ as seen in section 1.5, the size of the result is in the order of $|\mathcal{A}_1| \times \cdots \times |\mathcal{A}_n|$, that is, potentially exponential with respect to the system description.

Even more frequently, such explosions arise whenever we deal with interpreted automata, for example with automata operating on state variables. To the extent that the behavior (and perhaps some atomic propositions) depend on the values of the variables, the automaton $\mathcal{A}$ submitted to the model checker has to be the automaton of the configurations. For example, for an automaton having $m = |Q|$ control states and n merely boolean state variables, the model checker will be staring at an automaton having $m.2^n$ states.

When the system under study requires global states to remember values that are not *a priori* bounded (integers, a waiting queue, etc.) an automaton with an infinite number of states arises and the methods described here no longer apply [4].

---

[4] As already hinted at in chapter 1, there exist methods capable of automatically verifying certain classes of such automata: these methods are far beyond the scope of this book and we will merely refer to these indirectly and incompletely, for example in the third part of the book, when discussing tools.

4. Symbolic Model Checking

Generally speaking, *symbolic model checking* refers to any model checking method which would attempt to represent symbolically (as opposed to "explicitly") the states and transitions of an automaton targeted for verification. We often use this term, as well, to refer to a particular symbolic method in which *Binary Decision Diagrams* (BDD) are used to represent the state variables.

We saw earlier (see section 3.3) that state explosion is the main problem encountered by the model checking algorithms for CTL or PLTL. This explosion occurs whenever we choose to list and explicitly represent in memory all the states of the automaton under study.

The idea underlying symbolic methods is to be able to represent very large sets of states concisely and to manipulate them, as if they were in bulk. We note that such an approach becomes less dependent on the finiteness of the total number of states so that it applies equally well to infinite state systems (for example automata equipped with unbounded channels, or integer variables or clocks with values in $\mathbb{R}$, or using dynamic parallelism, etc.)

In this chapter, we first present (in section 4.1) the *iterative computation of state sets* method. This is the starting point of symbolic model checking methods, and it is important to understand why these methods essentially apply to the logic CTL.

Then we describe (from section 4.2 onwards) a particular BDD-based symbolic method which was proved successful for the verification of very large systems.

4.1 Symbolic Computation of State Sets

Iterative computation of $Sat(\phi)$. Let $\mathcal{A} = \langle Q, T, \ldots \rangle$ be an automaton. For a set $S \subseteq Q$ of its states, $Pre(S)$ stands for the set of immediate predecessors (in $\mathcal{A}$) of the states belonging to S. For a CTL formula ϕ, denote by $Sat(\phi)$ the set of states of $\mathcal{A}$ which satisfy ϕ. The semantics of CTL (given in section 2.3) allows us to express $Sat(\phi)$ in terms of the *Pre* operator and of the sets $Sat(\psi_i)$ for the sub-formulas ψ_i of ϕ.

Computing $Sat(\phi)$ can now be done as follows:

$$
\begin{aligned}
Sat(\neg\psi) &= Q \setminus Sat(\psi) \\
Sat(\psi \wedge \psi') &= Sat(\psi) \cap Sat(\psi') \\
Sat(\mathsf{EX}\psi) &= Pre(Sat(\psi)) \\
Sat(\mathsf{AX}\psi) &= Q \setminus Pre(Q \setminus Sat(\psi)) \\
Sat(\mathsf{EF}\psi) &= Pre^*(Sat(\psi))
\end{aligned}
$$
$$\cdots$$

The notation $Q \setminus X$ represents the complement of a subset X of Q. For $Sat(\mathsf{EF}\psi)$, we have used the notation $Pre^*(S)$ to represent the set of predecessors of S in the broad sense, that is *predecessors in zero, one or more steps*. We can compute $Pre^*(S)$ from Pre using iteration:

```
/* ===== Computation of Pre*(S) (for Sat[EF psi]) ===== */
X := S;
Y := {};
while (Y != X) {          /* Y is not a fixed point */
  Y := X;
  X := X \/ Pre(X);       /* \/ = set union */
}
return X;
```

Termination is guaranteed if we assume finiteness of $\mathcal{A}$.

For temporal combinators more complicated than EF, it is still possible to perform an iterative computation based on Pre. Actually, all CTL combinators can be handled by such computations, on the grounds that temporal combinators can be defined as fixed points [EC80]. Consider for example $\mathsf{A}\psi_1\mathsf{U}\psi_2$. From the equivalence

$$\mathsf{A}\psi_1\mathsf{U}\psi_2 \equiv \psi_2 \vee \left(\psi_1 \wedge \mathsf{EX}\ \mathsf{true} \wedge \mathsf{AX}(\mathsf{A}\psi_1\mathsf{U}\psi_2)\right)$$

we extract the algorithm:

```
/* ====== Computation of Sat[A psi1 U psi2] ====== */
P1 := Sat[psi1];
P2 := Sat[psi2];
X := P2;
Y := {};
while (Y != X) {        /* not yet stabilized */
  Y := X;               /* /\ = set intersection */
  X := X \/ (P1 /\ Pre(Q) /\ (Q \ Pre(Q \ X)));
}
return X;
```

It is possible to view the algorithm from section 3.1 as a particular implementation of a $Sat(\phi)$ computation. In this view, the sets $Sat(\psi)$ are represented by the marks $q.psi = true$ on the graph. This representation is largely equivalent to an explicit representation (or *enumerative*, or *extensive*) of the state sets. By opposition, symbolic model checking uses *symbolic representations* for the state sets. It then computes $Sat(\phi)$ by manipulating these symbolic notations.

Which symbolic representations to use. Take the example of an automaton $\mathcal{A}$ involving two variables declared as var a,b:0..255. The states of our automaton are then triples $\langle q, v, v' \rangle$ where q is a control state and v and v' are bytes corresponding to the values of a and b, so that $Q_{\mathcal{A}}$ contains many tens of thousands of states! We could choose to represent the set $Q_{\mathcal{A}}$ by the expression $\langle *, *, * \rangle$. In a similar way, the symbolic notation $\langle q_2, 3, * \rangle$ would represent the set of triples $\langle q, v, v' \rangle$ such that q equals q_2, v equals 3, and v' is arbitrary. Each of these encodings concisely represents a part of $Q_{\mathcal{A}}$.

It would be possible to use such a notation (which would of course require a complete formalization) to represent the sets of our automaton states. If we wish to use these in order to implement the iterative computation of $Sat(\phi)$, it is necessary to have access to the following primitives:

1. a symbolic representation of $Sat(P)$ for each proposition $P \in Prop$,
2. an algorithm to compute (a symbolic representation of) $Pre(S)$ from a symbolic representation of S,
3. algorithms to compute the complement, the union and the intersection of the symbolic representations of the sets,
4. an algorithm to tell whether two symbolic representations represent the same set.

Operation 4 is necessary in order to implement the stabilization test required to detect termination of the iterative computation. Equality testing reduces to testing emptiness when the set operations of item 3 are available.

Note that items 3 and 4 are intrinsic properties of the representation system chosen for the sets. Items 1 and 2 also depend on this representation but they depend as well on the way in which the automaton and its transitions have been defined.

Let us return to our example automaton $\mathcal{A}$. The notation $\langle q_2, 3, * \rangle$ is clear, but how is the complement of $\langle q_2, 3, * \rangle$ represented? And how do we compute the complement in general? We see that we must extend our notation system, for example by introducing the apparatus allowing to write the complement of $\langle q_2, 3, * \rangle$ as $\langle q_1, *, * \rangle + \langle q_2, [0; 2], * \rangle + \langle q_2, [4; 255], * \rangle + \langle q_3, *, * \rangle$ (assuming the control states to be q_1, q_2, q_3). It remains for us to develop efficient algorithms to manipulate these representations.

We must also know how to compute $Pre(S)$. If the transitions are given by simple arithmetic instructions limited to increments and decrements of the variables a and b, then $Pre(S)$ will be relatively easy to compute. For example, for the automaton `var a,b:0..255;`

we could compute $Pre(\langle q_1, [100; 250], [8; 109]\rangle)$ and discover that the latter is the set represented by $\langle q_1, [110; 255], [8; 109]\rangle$. If the automaton also contained transitions labelled by `a := a*b` (or simply `a := a+b`) the computation of $Pre(S)$ would become much more subtle.

We thus see why a specific symbolic notation system often assumes that the automaton transitions obey some rather strict constraints.

Which logic for symbolic model checking. The logics based on state formulas are those which best lend themselves to symbolic model checking. Examples are CTL, and also the mu-calculus on trees [Koz83]. These logics are well adapted to the writing of iterative algorithms for $Sat(\phi)$. Nevertheless, stabilization can be very slow when the iterations involve loops and nested tests. For that reason, we prefer restricting ourselves to CTL (or to the *alternation-free* mu-calculus on trees).

The method presented above (section 3.2) for model checking PLTL can be expressed in terms of the iterative computation of $Sat(\psi_i)$, once $\mathcal{B}_{\neg\phi}$ is explicitly constructed and is synchronized with the automaton under study (without an intermediate unfolding step). This approach however is not commonly used in practice.

Systems with infinitely many states. The symbolic approach naturally extends to infinite systems. In our example, we could easily imagine that our two counters are *unbounded* integers and could allow us to write e.g. $\langle q, [100; \infty[, [8; 109]\rangle$ for unbounded intervals.

In general, symbolic model checking for infinite systems is faced with two new difficulties:

- first, it becomes much trickier to come up with symbolic representations for which the set operations are computable [1];
- second, the iterative computation of $Sat(\phi)$ is no longer guaranteed to terminate (to reach the stabilization point, also called fixed point), and this computation in general has no reason to end.

Thus, in our example of the automaton with unbounded counters a and b, the set of states from which $\langle q_2, 0, 0\rangle$ is reachable contains all the $\langle q_1, v, v'\rangle$ *in which v is a multiple of* 10, but the iterative computation of $Sat(\mathsf{EF}(v = v' = 0))$ will not terminate. Incidentally, it is not possible to represent the set $Sat(\mathsf{EF}(v = v' = 0))$ in the simple open intervals notation used in the bounded case.

---

[1] That is, have the property that an algorithm exists to implement them, in the sense of computability theory.

4.2 Binary Decision Diagrams (BDD)

A *BDD* is a particular data structure which is very commonly used for the symbolic representation of state sets. Bryant [Bry86, Bry92] has popularized their use, and their application to model checking was suggested by three different groups [CBM90, BCM$^+$92, Pix92].

In practice, BDDs have made possible the verification of systems which could never have been constructed explicitly (unfolded) for the purposes of verification by the enumerative approach.

BDDs combine several advantages:

Efficiency: basic operations (intersection, complement, comparison, projection, etc.) are cheap, that is, linear or quadratic, even instantaneous (case of the equality test). The data structure is very compact (low memory requirements in general).

Simplicity: the data structure and the associated algorithms are simple to describe and to implement.

Easy adaptation: BDDs are appropriate for problems dealing with rather loosely correlated data, which is often the case for state variables in an automaton, and *a fortiori* in automata arranged as a network.

Generality: BDDs are not tied to a particular family of automata but they provide an easy representation for all kinds of finite systems.

We will first present BDDs and the associated manipulations. Then, in section 4.4, we will explain how they are used for model checking in CTL.

BDD structure. Consider n boolean variables $x_1, \ldots, x_n$. A tuple $\langle b_1, \ldots, b_n \rangle$ associates a boolean value b_i with each x_i. We wish to represent a set of such tuples. For example, suppose that $n = 4$ and that the set of interest is the set S of all the tuples $\langle b_1, b_2, b_3, b_4 \rangle$ such that $(b_1 \vee b_3) \wedge (b_2 \Rightarrow b_4)$ is true. S contains 9 tuples. We can imagine many ways to represent this set: by enumeration of its 9 elements $S = \{\langle F, F, T, F \rangle, \ldots\}$, by the boolean formula $(b_1 \vee b_3) \wedge (b_2 \Rightarrow b_4)$ itself, and by a boolean formula in disjunctive normal form $(b_1 \wedge \neg b_2) \vee (b_1 \wedge b_4) \vee (b_3 \wedge \neg b_2) \vee (b_3 \wedge b_4)$.

We can also represent S by means of a *decision tree* like in figure 4.1. Such a tree allows us to determine whether a given tuple $\langle b_1, b_2, b_3, b_4 \rangle$ belongs to S. Starting from the root n_1, we choose the left son, n_2, or the right son, n_3, according to whether b_1 is F or T, then we continue according to the value of b_2, etc. At the end, the tuple belongs to S if and only if we reach a leaf labelled T (we can also view the tree as a *boolean function* associating T or F with each tuple).

Each representation has its advantages and its drawbacks. Moreover, each representation naturally leads to a data structure which promotes or hinders algorithmic efficiency. When it comes to determining whether a given n-tuple is in S, the decision tree delivers an answer in n time units. The other representations require time proportional to the representation itself, whose size

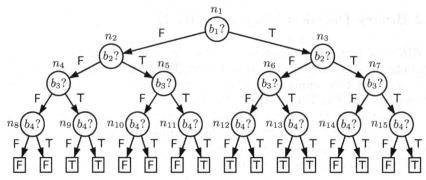

Fig. 4.1. A decision tree for $(b_1 \lor b_3) \land (b_2 \Rightarrow b_4)$

can be exponential in n. As to the decision tree, its size is always exponential, which is its main drawback.

Decision tree reduction. A BDD is a *reduced decision tree*. The reductions obey two very precise rules:

1. First, identical subtrees are identified and shared. In the example on figure 4.1, the subtree out of n_8 is identical to that out of n_{10} (in fact the 8 nodes n_8 to n_{15} belong to three distinct types only). Such identifications are possible at all levels. The sharing of identical subtrees destroys the tree structure and leads to the creation of a directed acyclic graph (or *dag*).

2. Second, superfluous internal nodes are deleted (a node is superfluous if it corresponds to no real choice, in the manner that its left and right sons are identical). In the example on figure 4.1, the node n_7 is superfluous. The test on b_3 is therefore useless in that part of the tree.

Figure 4.2 depicts the BDD obtained by reducing the tree from figure 4.1. This BDD can also be used to determine whether a tuple belongs to the set S, with essentially the same choice procedure between left and right sons. It may now happen that some components of the tuple need not even be consulted.

The reduction yields its first advantage: it makes the representation smaller. Symbolic representations based on boolean expressions also allow such space savings, but a second advantage of BDDs is their canonicity.

Canonicity of BDDs. The fundamental property of BDDs is that they *canonically* represent sets of boolean tuples: *if the order of the variables x_i is fixed, then there exists a unique BDD for each set S* [Bry92].

The order referred to is the order in which the variables are examined as we proceed down a path in the BDD or the decision tree. In the sequel we will assume this order to be fixed: b_1 before b_2 before b_3 etc.

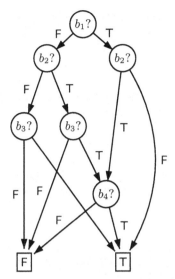

Fig. 4.2. The BDD resulting from reducing the tree on figure 4.1

We can then test the equivalence of two symbolic representations in constant time [2], which is impossible for boolean expressions. In particular, it is possible to tell whether a BDD represents the empty set simply by verifying whether it is reduced to a unique leaf F.

Operations on BDDs. All the boolean operations can be implemented efficiently on BDDs:

Emptiness test: a BDD represents an empty set if and only if it is reduced to the single leaf F.

Comparison: two BDDs represent the same set if and only if they are identical.

Complementation: if the BDD B represents S, then the complement of S is represented by B', a BDD obtained from B by replacing the T leaf by a F leaf and vice versa.

Intersection: it is obtained by a slightly more complicated algorithm. If B_1 and B_2 represent the sets S_1 and S_2 respectively, we can construct a BDD B for $S_1 \cap S_2$. The idea is to compute, for each pair (n_1, n_2) formed of a B_1 node and a B_2 node, the node $n_1 \cap n_2$ of B corresponding to their conjunction.

Suppose that n_1 has the form "if b_1 then n_1' else n_1''" and that n_2 has the form "if b_2 then n_2' else n_2''". If $b_1 = b_2$, $n_1 \cap n_2$ is "if b_1 then $n_1' \cap n_2'$, else $n_1'' \cap n_2''$". If b_1 appears before b_2 in the ordering, $n_1 \cap n_2$ is "if b_1 then

---

[2] If the identical subgraphs are identified at the time of their construction (for example using hashing methods), so that there never exist two distinct instances of one BDD.

$n'_1 \cap n_2$, else $n''_1 \cap n_2$" (and if b_1 appears after b_2, we argue by symmetry). The case of leaves is even simpler. It then remains to reduce the result, following the principles seen above. (This reduction is often performed while the BDD is being constructed. As well, we avoid systematically exploring all the pairs (n_1, n_2).)

We see that B will have a size at most $|B_1| \times |B_2|$, that is to say quadratic.

Union and the other binary boolean operations: we compute them like the intersection, at the same quadratic cost.

Projections and abstractions: the projection $S[x_i := \mathsf{T}]$ consists in taking all the tuples of S and modifying them by assigning the T value to position i. The abstraction $\exists x_i.S$ gathers all the tuples (with $m = n - 1$) which can be completed, by the insertion of an appropriate value b_i for x_i, into a n-tuple of S.

These operations are quadratic in the worst case.

Let us stress that the linear or quadratic complexity applies to *one* set operation. A symbolic model checking computation may require cascading a great many such operations, and symbolic model checking suffers, like any other method, from the same combinatorial explosion risks on certain problems.

4.3 Representing Automata by BDDs

Before being able to apply the BDD technology to symbolic model checking, we need to restate the model checking problem in terms of boolean tuples. This requires an encoding representing the states and transitions of the automata under study.

Representing the states by BDDs. Consider the case of an automaton $\mathcal{A}$, with control state set $Q = \{q_0, \ldots, q_6\}$, involving an integer variable declared as var digit:0..9 and a boolean variable var ready:bool.

A state of $\mathcal{A}$ is then a triple $\langle q, k, b \rangle$, for example $\langle q_3, 8, \mathsf{F} \rangle$. We will represent each component using a boolean sequence, exactly as we would use an appropriate number of bits to encode in binary a number in a finite range. We will require three bits b_1^1, b_1^2, b_1^3 for $q \in Q$, four bits $b_2^1, b_2^2, b_2^3, b_2^4$ for $0 \le k \le 9$, and one bit b_3^1 for b. Thus $\langle q_3, 8, \mathsf{F} \rangle$ is represented by:

$$\langle \overbrace{\underset{b_1^1}{\mathsf{F}}, \underset{b_1^2}{\mathsf{T}}, \underset{b_1^3}{\mathsf{T}}}^{q_3}, \overbrace{\underset{b_2^1}{\mathsf{T}}, \underset{b_2^2}{\mathsf{F}}, \underset{b_2^3}{\mathsf{F}}, \underset{b_2^4}{\mathsf{F}}}^{8}, \underset{b_3^1}{\mathsf{F}} \rangle.$$

The BDD on figure 4.3 then represents the set $Sat(\texttt{ready} \Rightarrow (\texttt{digit} > 2))$ of states $\langle q, k, b \rangle$ such that if $b = \mathsf{T}$ then $k > 2$.

Note that the resulting BDD allows triples which do not correspond to any state $\langle q, k, b \rangle$ of $Q_\mathcal{A}$. Our encoding allows eight possible values for q and sixteen for k.

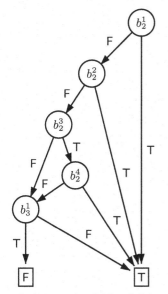

Fig. 4.3. The BDD of the states for which `ready` $\Rightarrow$ (`digit` > 2)

From a theoretical point of view, this surge in the number of states causes no problem: the superfluous states are unreachable and they will not affect the yes or no answer to a model checking question.

On the practical side, the surge is hardly a problem and once in a while it may even lead to a simplification of certain BDDs. Moreover, if we wish to do so, it is easy to guarantee that we only ever process tuples which truly correspond to states of $\mathcal{A}$, by intersecting each BDD with the BDD for $Q_{\mathcal{A}}$, the set of relevant tuples.

Representing transitions by BDDs. To represent the transitions of an automaton, the same idea is applied. A transition is a pair $\langle s, s' \rangle$ specifying a state and a target state. We will encode such pairs as n-tuples. The simplest way is to allocate twice the number of bits required to encode a state. The first half of the bits, the b_i^j, represents the start state s and the second, the $b_i'^j$, represents the target state s'. For example, the transition $\langle q_3, 8, \mathsf{F} \rangle \rightarrow \langle q_5, 0, \mathsf{F} \rangle$ turns into:

$$\langle \overbrace{\mathsf{F}}_{b_1^1}, \overbrace{\mathsf{T}}_{b_1^2}, \underbrace{\mathsf{T}}_{b_1^3}, \overbrace{\mathsf{T}}^{8}_{b_2^1}, \underbrace{\mathsf{F}}_{b_2^2}, \underbrace{\mathsf{F}}_{b_2^3}, \underbrace{\mathsf{F}}_{b_2^4}, \underbrace{\mathsf{F}}_{b_3^1}, \overbrace{\mathsf{T}}^{q_5}_{b_1'^1}, \underbrace{\mathsf{F}}_{b_1'^2}, \underbrace{\mathsf{T}}_{b_1'^3}, \overbrace{\mathsf{F}}^{0}_{b_2'^1}, \underbrace{\mathsf{F}}_{b_2'^2}, \underbrace{\mathsf{F}}_{b_2'^3}, \underbrace{\mathsf{F}}_{b_2'^4}, \underbrace{\mathsf{F}}_{b_3'^1} \rangle.$$

Following this scheme, the set T of $\mathcal{A}$ transitions is viewed as a set of tuples. It is easy to construct the associated BDD B_T. Say that our automaton involves the following transition:

$$q_1 \xrightarrow{\text{if } \mathtt{digit} \neq 0,\ \mathtt{ready} := \mathsf{T}} q_2$$

The set of pairs $(\langle q, k, b\rangle, \langle q', k', b'\rangle)$ corresponding to this transition contains all the pairs satisfying the condition:

$$q = q_1, k \neq 0, q' = q_2, k' = k \text{ and } b' = \mathsf{T}. \tag{4.1}$$

To obtain a BDD representing these pairs, it suffices to express (4.1) in terms of the bits encoding the state components:

$$\bigwedge \underbrace{\neg b_1^1 \wedge \neg b_1^2 \wedge b_1^3}_{q=q_1} \bigwedge \underbrace{(b_2^1 \vee b_2^2 \vee b_2^3 \vee b_2^4)}_{k\neq 0} \bigwedge \underbrace{\neg b'^1_1 \wedge b'^2_1 \wedge \neg b'^3_1}_{q'=q_2}$$

$$\underbrace{b'^1_2 \Leftrightarrow b_2^1 \wedge b'^2_2 \Leftrightarrow b_2^2 \wedge b'^3_2 \Leftrightarrow b_2^3 \wedge b'^4_2 \Leftrightarrow b_2^4}_{k'=k} \bigwedge \underbrace{b'^1_3}_{b'=\mathsf{T}}$$

This coding operation is easy to mechanize and it only requires the basic operations encountered in section 4.2.

4.4 BDD-based Model Checking

We have seen that BDDs often provide a compact representation for the sets of states of an automaton $\mathcal{A}$. This representation supports the basic set operations such as union, complement, and comparison. It can thus serve as a particular instance of the general symbolic model checking scheme presented in section 4.1.

Computation of $Pre(S)$. The only operation not yet explained, which is crucial to symbolic model checking, is the $Pre(S)$ computation, for a set S of states. This computation is very simple once the relation T is represented as a BDD B_T as described in section 4.3.

To explain the idea on an example, say that S corresponds to $q = q_1 \wedge k = 0$ and that T corresponds to $q = q_0 \wedge q' = q_1 \wedge k' = k$. Of course, S and T are given in BDD form as B_S and B_T. We begin by constructing a BDD B'_S in which each b_i^j in B_S is replaced by its copy b'^j_i. We thus obtain a *primed version of S*. In our example, B'_S corresponds to $q' = q_1 \wedge k' = 0$. B'_S is easily obtained in linear time.

We then compute $B_T \cap B'_S$. In our example we obtain a BDD corresponding to $q = q_0 \wedge q' = q_1 \wedge k' = k \wedge q' = q_1 \wedge k' = 0$, that is to say $q = q_0 \wedge q' = q_1 \wedge k = 0 \wedge k' = 0$. This in fact consists of the set of pairs (s, s') of T such that $s' \in S$.

It remains to apply the abstraction operation $\exists q' \exists k'$ which will delete any reference to the b'^j_i (but will retain the b_i^j) to obtain the BDD representing $Pre(S)$. In our example, we obtain a BDD corresponding to $q = q_0 \wedge k = 0$.

Implementation. The techniques which we have presented are implemented in tools like, for example, SMV (see chapter 12). In these tools, the efficiency of the BDDs may depend on subtle factors.

For example, for complicated systems, the construction of the BDD B_T representing the transition relation T can at times be the main obstacle: this owes to the fact that T contains *pairs of states* and is represented by a BDD on $2n$ boolean variables, as opposed to n for the BDDs representing the sets $Sat(\phi)$. The risk of combinatorial explosion then runs high, and it can prove wise to build separately the relations $B_{T_1}, \ldots, B_{T_m}$ corresponding to natural subsets of transitions of the automaton, for example one T_i for each transition of the automaton before its unfolding. We then compute $Pre(S)$ as $Pre[T_1](S) \cup \cdots \cup Pre[T_m](S)$.

The choice of ordering for the boolean variables is equally crucial. For example, the start and target states of a transition often share common variables. This occurs in the example (4.1) above, where $k' = k$. More generally, this situation is encountered whenever the automaton under study involves variables. Similarly, in a network of synchronized automata, a transition frequently only modifies the local state of a single automaton in the network, leaving the others unchanged.

In terms of BDDs, this leads to relations verifying $b_i^j \Leftrightarrow b_i'^j$ for many boolean variables. The BDDs corresponding to these transition relations will instantly grow to exponential size if the ordering of the boolean variables does not position each b_i^j in the immediate vicinity of (for example immediately before) the corresponding $b_i'^j$. With such a judicious ordering (which remains to be completed), a fifteen node BDD can represent the relation corresponding to (4.1).

Nevertheless, BDDs have only pushed the limit of what could be achieved. BDDs can themselves become inadequate rather quickly. To see this, it suffices to consider a system such as that presented in section 1.5 combining several counters having periods $p_1, \ldots, p_k$. Such a system possesses $N = p_1 \times \ldots \times p_k$ states and every state is reachable from any other in at most N steps. This maximum may be necessary and in such a case the iterative computation of the $Pre^i(\{q_0\})$ will give rise to N BDDs before it stabilizes. Otherwise stated, an exponential number of BDDs will be generated which, being all distinct, will use up an exponential amount of memory.

Perspectives. The previous sections demonstrated that BDDs provide all the basic ingredients to a symbolic model checker. In fact, such tools appeared as early as in 1990. The models based on synchronized automata, which manipulate variables having a finite range, are good candidates for model checking using this approach, and it has been possible to verify large size systems (requiring over a hundred boolean variables to represent the states).

Current work on model checking classifies schematically into two broad categories: work aimed at applying BDD technology to solve more verification problems (for example, program equivalence), and work aimed at developing techniques potentially able to extend the limits inherent to BDD-based model checking.

Fortunately, these inherent BDD limits are sufficiently remote, nowadays, for symbolic model checking to have secured its relevance and for its techniques to find almost systematic use throughout the VLSI design industry.

5. Timed Automata

As we have seen in chapter 1, classical automata can model the sequencing of the actions in a network, for example "trigger the `alarm` action upon detection of a `problem`". This temporal sequencing *conveys no quantitative information on the delay between two actions*. It is therefore not possible to directly model the triggering of an alarm *less than 5 seconds after* detecting a problem. But such constraints, which we can refer to as "real-time", are often an essential part of the modeling of reactive systems.

In practice, this limitation is often circumvented by the use of a global clock controlling the actions of a network of automata. We add to the usual automata some special transitions, representing "clock ticks" which monitor the passage of time: by synchronizing the various automata in the network on these transitions, we make sure that all the automata evolve at the same speed. The time interval between the two actions then corresponds to the number of "tick" transitions performed between them.

This type of solution is blatantly inadequate. First, it requires adding a very cumbersome encoding method to measure time intervals, which reduces the readability of the model and renders handling and updating the model much trickier and prone to errors. Second, it blurs the distinction between the two categories of system transitions: those which correspond to time elapsing and those which modify the control state. Thus, replacing a procedure "Wait for 10 seconds" by "Wait for 100 seconds", or even "Wait for 20 half-seconds", entails an overhaul of the underlying structure of the relevant automata. Obviously, the abstraction level of such a construction is too low. Ensuring that the model obtained is faithful to the system being modeled becomes difficult.

Timed automata were proposed (by Alur and Dill [AD94]) as an answer to this precise need to integrate, by means of a distinct mechanism, quantitative information on the passage of time in automata. Timed automata allow us for example (i) to state that a given automaton will not remain longer than 3 minutes in a given control state and (ii) to modify the value of the constant 3 at a later time, without having to transform the model structure.

5.1 Description of a Timed Automaton

A timed automaton is built from Two fundamental elements:

- a finite automaton in the usual sense, which describes the system control states and the transitions, assumed instantaneous, between these states;
- clocks (or chronometers), used to specify the quantitative time constraints, which may be associated with the transitions.

In this model the transitions remain instantaneous as in everything we have seen thus far. The great benefit of this viewpoint is to preserve the simple semantics of the actions. The "time" on which we reason elapses only between transitions. If we wish to speak of the *duration of an action a*, it is possible to break it up into two distinct actions: the beginning of *a* and its end.

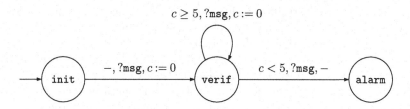

Fig. 5.1. A timed automaton

An example. The timed automaton on figure 5.1 models a system which triggers an alarm when a delay between the reception of two messages (represented by the transitions ?msg) is less than 5 seconds. This automaton uses a clock c. We start from the state init with c set to 0. The value of c increases with time. When the first message is received, we move on to state verif and reset clock c. From this point on, the clock increases again with time.

When a message is next received, either the value of c is at least 5 and we remain in state verif and reset c to zero, or c is less than 5 and we move on to the alarm state. We see that the guards $c \geq 5$ and $c < 5$ of the two transitions out of the state verif take care of this test. (Note that the if keyword is omitted within timed automata guards.)

Clocks and transitions. Clocks are variables having non-negative real values (we denote by $\mathbb{R}$ the set of real numbers). In the initial system state, all clock values are null: they then all evolve at the same speed, synchronously with time.

Besides the source and target states, three items are associated with a transition:

1. A *guard*, also called *firing condition*, involving the clock values. For example the alarm transition on figure 5.1 has guard $c < 5$ and the transition from init to verif has no condition(the guard is true).
2. A label, or action name, as usual (?msg in the above example).
3. *reset* of some clocks, for example $c := 0$ on figure 5.1.

Of course, a given transition can only occur if the associated condition holds for the current values of the clocks. In fact, since a clock c can be reset when firing a transition, its value at time t measures the delay between t and the latest time at which c was reset. Clocks therefore measure time intervals and, in any particular system, many clocks could be necessary to measure delays which are independent from each other.

The system thus operates as if equipped with a global clock that measures the time ; each individual clock is synchronized within this system from the moment they are reset at zero.

Configurations and executions. At any time, the configuration (or global state) of the system is given by (i) the current control state of the automaton and (ii) the value of each clock.

We write (q, v) for such a configuration, with q a control state of the automaton, and v a mapping associating with each clock its current value (a real number). We refer to v as a *valuation* of the automaton clocks.

The system configuration changes in two ways:

• by letting a time delay $d \in \mathbb{R}$ elapse: the values of all the clocks then increase by d, leading to a valuation which we simply write as $v + d$. We then move on from (q, v) to $(q, v + d)$. We speak of a *delay* transition;
• by activating the automaton, that is by carrying out a firable transition: the clocks to be reset then take on the value zero, the values of the other clocks remain unchanged. We then speak of a *discrete transition*, or sometimes of an *action transition*.

For example, starting from the configuration (init, 0), the timed automaton on figure 5.1 may evolve as follows:

$$(\text{init}, 0) \rightarrow (\text{init}, 10.2) \overset{?\text{msg}}{\rightarrow} (\text{verif}, 0) \rightarrow (\text{verif}, 5.8) \overset{?\text{msg}}{\rightarrow} (\text{verif}, 0)$$
$$\rightarrow (\text{verif}, 3.1) \overset{?\text{msg}}{\rightarrow} (\text{alarm}, 3.1) \cdots$$

The first transition corresponds to a time lapse of 10.2 seconds, the third to a delay of 5.8 seconds and the fifth to a delay of 3.1 seconds. We speak of "seconds" because the guard $c \geq 5$ was written to express the fact that each new message arrives at least *5 seconds* after the preceding one. The timed automaton model of course does not fix the time unit under consideration.

An execution of a timed automaton is therefore a (usually infinite) sequence of configurations where two successive configurations correspond either to an action, or to a time delay.

Executions and trajectories. Except for a few details, an execution of a timed automaton can be viewed as a mapping ρ from $\mathbb{R}_+$ to the set of configurations (the set of pairs (q, v)). We can also speak of *trajectory*, as in physics. The initial state is $\rho(0)$, and $\rho(t)$ is the configuration at time t along this execution. For example, for the above execution ρ, $\rho(12.3) = (\mathtt{verif}, 2.1)$ since the instant 12.3 occurs after the execution of the first message.

The trajectory viewpoint correspond to a global time outside the system, whereas the valuations notion affords a more local viewpoint, internal to the system. Note that a run of a timed automaton allows us to cascade several discrete transitions with no intervening delay. The various configurations encountered in such a sequence are then associated with a single global date which cannot be taken into account by the notion of trajectory.

5.2 Networks of Timed Automata and Synchronization

As in the case of untimed automata, the ability to build a timed model in a composite fashion, by combining several parallel automata synchronized with one another, is very useful. Such synchronized automata then constitute a *timed automata network*.

Executions of a timed automata network. As always, a network execution is a (possibly infinite) sequence of configurations, but a network configuration now includes the current control state of each of the automata and the value of clocks. As before, a configuration can change in two ways:

- if there is a time delay of d: the values of *all clocks* increase by d ;
- by performing an action corresponding to a firable transition in one of the component automata (or a synchronization of such actions): only the current state of the relevant component(s) can change. The clock values evolve as before: they are either reset, or unchanged.

Thus, all automata components run in parallel at the same speed. Their clocks are all synchronized to the same global clock. It is no problem to permit the sharing of clocks between the different automata of the network. Or rather, the problems which arise are the same as for any other shared variable. The overwriting of the variable by one of the components (it being reset in the case of clocks) can have unforeseen effects on the behavior of the remaining components.

Here as well we use the notation (q, v) to refer to the network configuration: q then represents a control state vector and v is a function associating with each network clock its value at the current time.

Synchronization. As in the standard case, timed automata synchronize on transitions. Assume that a network of three automata is in the configuration

(q_1, q_2, q_3, v) and that a_1, a_2, a_3 of these automata (firable in this configuration) are synchronized. If these actions are performed, they are then simultaneous and produce in one step a new configuration (q'_1, q'_2, q'_3, v'). The valuation v' differs from v only in the clocks reset to zero by the transitions a_1, a_2 and a_3; the clocks which were not reset are unchanged. Note that, since reset writes a zero value and nothing else, there are no concurrent write conflicts.

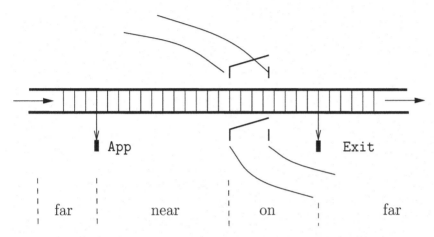

Fig. 5.2. A railway crossing

Example: modeling a railway crossing. Figure 5.2 depicts a railway crossing involving a gate, and two sensors App and Exit respectively telling the gate that a train is approaching and leaving the passageway. This is a classical example of a real-time system, which we will only model very coarsely [1] here, assuming that there is only a single train and the gate.

If the train speed on this railway section and the opening and closing speeds of the gate are known, then it is possible to model this system with the two timed automata on figure 5.3. To simplify, we assume the time unit is a minute. Synchronization is performed on the actions shared by the two automata: App and Exit. The internal transitions (unlabelled) are not synchronized.

The automaton modeling the train can switch from state **far** to **near** by emitting the App signal and must synchronize with the corresponding transition (also labelled App) in the automaton modeling the gate. The gate automaton then enters the state **lower** if its state was **up**, then the train spends two to five minutes reaching the crossing, etc.

---

[1] We will propose richer models for this example in the chapters devoted to model checkers for timed systems.

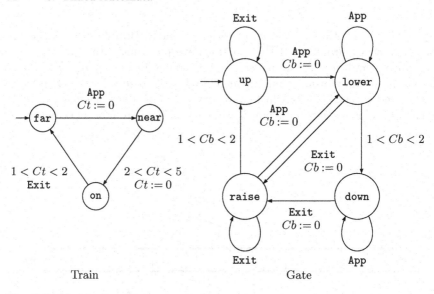

Fig. 5.3. Model of a railway crossing

The gate can be up, down, or in intermediate situations (in the process of going up or coming down). We assume that it needs between one and two minutes to go up (to go from the state **down** to the state **up**) or to come down: this information is represented by the guards on the internal transitions. Furthermore, each state of the "gate" automaton is equipped with transitions **App** and **Exit** corresponding to the reception of the signals emitted by the train. These signals represent sensors, they are "*uncontrolled signals*" and the gate must be in a position, regardless of its current state, to receive them and to act accordingly.

5.3 Variants and Extensions of the Basic Model

Other models of timed automata exist in the literature. Those that are more restrictive than the model presented in this book are essentially justified by their greater likelihood of being able to support automatic verification. Unfortunately these more restrictive models cannot be combined into synchronized networks, which explains our choice of model in this book.

In addition, timed automata are often extended by such constructs aimed at simplifying the modeling. Obviously, adding discrete variables is very useful, as we have seen in the general untimed context (section 1.4). Here we present three other extensions, specific to the timed framework. Adding *invariants* and *urgent transitions* does not fundamentally change the basic model. *Hybrid systems* represent a much more significant extension.

Invariants. The firing conditions associated with transitions implement a notion of *possibility*: given a configuration, a transition corresponding to an action is enabled or disabled depending on the values of the clocks and variables. In general a system description also involves notions of *necessity* (of *liveness*) to ensure that certain transitions will indeed occur, otherwise a possible course of action would merely be to wait forever without ever performing a discrete transition. Note that, in the untimed model, this problem was alleviated by the simple fact that we consider *maximal* executions: there in disguise lies the liveness hypothesis. In timed systems, this solution no longer suffices.

For example it would be wise to guarantee the liveness of the automata on figure 5.3 if we wish to model in any meaningful way the railroad reality! Indeed, remaining in state **far** and state **up** for the train and gate respectively is no problem, but remaining in state **near** and state **down** indefinitely is unrealistic.

In general, to guarantee that certain transitions will occur, we associate with each control state q of the automata a condition on the clock values, called an *invariant*, which must always hold when the current state is q. In the case of a network, a configuration is *enabled* if the clock values satisfy the invariant of each current state in each automaton forming the network.

Thus, time can only flow as long as current invariants are fulfilled. Before the end of this delay, the system must necessarily trigger a discrete transition and reach a new enabled configuration. If no enabled configuration is reachable, the system faces a timed version of deadlock.

In the example on figure 5.3, we can add invariants to the "Train" and "Gate" automata so as to ensure that the train will remain indefinitely neither in the state **near** (invariant: $Ht < 5$), nor in the state **on** (invariant: $Ht < 2$) and that the gate will not remain in the states **raise** or **lower** (invariant : $Hb < 2$).

Urgency. In some situations, a notion of *urgent transition*, which cannot tolerate a time delay is useful.

Suppose, for example, that we wish to model the following system: two computations (**c1** and **c2**) are performed in parallel (each requiring less than two seconds), and *as soon as* these two computations end, a final computation **c3** is needed. One solution is to use the automata depicted on the figure 5.4, where we have chosen to synchronize the **c3** actions and declared them urgent (indicated on the diagram by dotted lines). This transition will be performed *as soon as* the two transitions **c1** and **c2** will have occurred because, upon the enabling of the transition **c3**, time can no longer flow.

Formally, if in a network of timed automata, an urgent transition can be performed, then time delays are forbidden: the network must perform a discrete transition, for example the urgent transition itself, but maybe yet another. Thus, it is actually the current configuration which represents an urgency situation, not the transition itself.

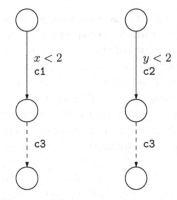

Fig. 5.4. Making use of urgent actions

This notion of urgency, though it adds no expressive power to automata networks, allows modeling some behaviors in a more natural way.

Hybrid linear systems. Hybrid systems are a natural generalization of timed automata, designed to provide access to *dynamic variables*. While clocks evolve at the rate of time, dynamic variables evolve (continuously) at different speeds. These variables could in fact represent altitude, temperature, speed, level, etc., even clock values (which can then be exact or drift).

Hybrid systems extend timed automata, designed to provide access to dynamic variables. In a hybrid automaton, with each control state is associated a law of evolution with respect to time (for example in the form of a differential equation) for each variable.

A particularly important case consists of *hybrid linear systems* which associate with each control state and each variable x an interval $[m_x, M_x]$ bounding the possible values of the derivative $\dot{x}$ of x with respect to time (with respect to the reference clock). Chapter 17 provides an example based on such systems for modeling a railway crossing.

We refer the interested reader to [ACHH93, ACH$^+$95, Hen96, HKPV98] for details on the verification of hybrid linear systems. Although many questions are undecidable in that framework, verification is sometimes possible, with an approach based on regions and zones, as is done for timed automata. Actually, the HyTech tool presented in chapter 17 adapts these techniques [ACH$^+$95].

Another widely used approach for the verification of hybrid linear systems involves their translation into timed automata [HKPV98]. This yields a special case of the abstraction methods presented in chapter 11.

5.4 Timed Temporal Logic

Given a system described as a network of timed automata, we wish to be able to state (and then verify) properties of this system. Among these properties, we find those that are simply temporal (for example "when the train is inside the crossing, the gate is always closed"), but also *real-time* properties which involve quantitative information on the delays between the actions. For example, we want to express that "the train always triggers an `Exit` signal within 7 minutes of having emitted an `App` signal".

To formally state such real-time properties, several tacks are possible. The simplest is to express the property in terms of the reachability (or the non-reachability) of some sets of configurations of the automaton.

For more complicated properties, we can also use the technique of *observer automata* encountered in section 3.2 in the context of model checking for linear-time logics [2]: given a property ϕ and a network R, we add to R a new automaton $\mathcal{A}_\phi$ synchronized over certain actions of R. Verifying ϕ is then reduced to testing reachability of some states in the product $R \parallel \mathcal{A}_\phi$. This method is often used in the tools UPPAAL (see chapter 15) and HYTECH (see chapter 17).

Another option is to use a *timed logic*, which is an extension or adaptation of a temporal logic by primitives expressing conditions on durations and dates. This approach is surely more satisfactory to the extent that it provides a *logical language* to specify the timed properties.

TCTL, *a timed version of* CTL. A very natural step is to extend the U, F, ..., operators from temporal logic with quantitative information on the flow of time, as initially proposed by R. Koymans [Koy90]. For instance, formula $PU_{<2}Q$ states that P is true until Q becomes true, and that Q will become true within two time units (of the current time).

Applied to CTL, this approach leads to a timed branching temporal logic: TCTL, or "Timed CTL".

The TCTL formulas are given by the following grammar:

$$
\begin{aligned}
\phi, \psi ::= &P_1 \mid P_2 \mid \dots && \text{(atomic propositions)} \\
&\mid \neg\phi \mid \phi \wedge \psi \mid \phi \Rightarrow \psi \mid \dots && \text{(boolean combinators)} \\
&\mid \mathsf{EF}_{(\sim k)}\phi \mid \mathsf{EG}_{(\sim k)}\phi \mid \mathsf{E}\phi\mathsf{U}_{(\sim k)}\psi && \text{(temporal combinators)} \\
&\mid \mathsf{AF}_{(\sim k)}\phi \mid \mathsf{AG}_{(\sim k)}\phi \mid \mathsf{A}\phi\mathsf{U}_{(\sim k)}\psi
\end{aligned}
$$

where $\sim$ is any comparison symbol drawn from $\{<, \leq, =, \geq, >\}$ and k is any rational number [3] from $\mathbb{Q}$. Note that, even though the duration of a delay transition can be a real number, the description language of the automata

---

[2] See also section 11.6.

[3] That is to say any fraction of two integers, like for example $\frac{8}{1000}$. In our examples we will only use integers: for a given timed automaton one can get rid of all the fractions by changing the time unit.

and the logic TCTL only express integer or rational constraints on these real values.

For example, a configuration satisfies $\mathsf{E}\phi\mathsf{U}_{(\leq 3)}\psi$ if there exists a trajectory ρ (an execution) out of this configuration and an instant $t \leq 3$ such that $\rho(t) \models \psi$ and $\rho(t') \models \phi$ for each $t' < t$. This is nothing but the usual CTL semantics with the additional condition that $t' \sim k$ (here $t' \leq 3$).

The CTL operators $\mathsf{E\_U\_}$ and $\mathsf{A\_U\_}$ correspond to the TCTL operators $\mathsf{E\_U}_{\geq 0\_}$ and $\mathsf{A\_U}_{\geq 0\_}$. Note that operator X does not exist in TCTL, because a notion of "next configuration" does not have the usual meaning when the clocks have real values.

The atomic propositions dealt with by the formulas of TCTL could include tests on the values of the automaton clocks. For example, we could imagine using the formula $\mathsf{AG}(h < 5)$ to check that the system clock h always has a value less than 5. The inclusion of this type of propositions would not affect the results which we are about to describe. On the other hand, this choice would be questionable because it is important to specify the system from a high level of abstraction without tying ourselves down to implementation details. From this point of view, the $\mathsf{E\_U}_{(\sim k)\_}$ and $\mathsf{A\_U}_{(\sim k)\_}$ operators are particularly interesting because they allow us to state real-time properties without reference to the automaton clocks.

The logic TCTL can express some real-time properties, for example:

- $\mathsf{AG}(\mathtt{pb} \Rightarrow \mathsf{AG}_{(\leq 5)}\mathtt{alarm})$ states that "if a problem occurs, then the alarm will sound immediately and it will sound for at least 5 time units";
- $\mathsf{AG}(\neg\mathtt{far} \Rightarrow \mathsf{AF}_{(<7)}\mathtt{far})$ states (in the railway crossing example), that "when the train is located in the railway section between the two sensors $\mathtt{App}$ and $\mathtt{Exit}$, it will leave this section before 7 time units".

5.5 Timed Model Checking

With timed automata and the logic TCTL in hand, we wish to obtain a model checking algorithm able to automatically decide whether some formula holds for a timed automaton (or a network).

In this context, the obvious difficulty is that a timed automaton has an infinite number of configurations, because there exist infinitely many possible clock valuations. This infiniteness has two sources: (1) the clock values are unbounded, and (2) even when restricted to a bounded interval, the set of real numbers is dense. Thus, the algorithm suggested for model checking CTL does not apply.

The idea to overcome this difficulty can be easily described intuitively: starting from two configurations (q, v) and (q, v') where v and v' are very close (for example $v(x) = 1.234066$ and $v'(x) = 1.23522$), a timed automaton will behave in roughly the same way and the two resulting configurations will verify the same TCTL formulas (assuming a notion of closeness for configurations is properly defined as a function of the formulas of interest). Also v and v' can be considered "close" when they are both beyond the constants handled by the timed automaton.

The idea of "closeness" is formally defined by an equivalence relation. Given the type of clock constraints appearing in the transitions and the largest constant used in these constraints, this equivalence $\sim$ on the clock valuations is defined with the following property: for any timed automaton using these constraints, two configurations (q, v) and (q, v') with $v \sim v'$ satisfy the same TCTL formulas. For timed automata [4] the number of equivalence classes, called *regions*, luckily happens to be finite.

Example. Figure 5.5 represents the set of regions for two clocks where we are only interested in constraints of the form $x \sim k$ with $x \in \{x_1, x_2\}$ and $k = 0, 1, 2$ for x_1, $k = 0, 1$ for x_2. In this example, there are 28 regions. Two configurations belonging to the same region are "close".

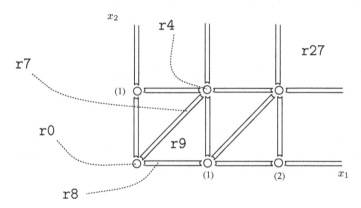

Fig. 5.5. Regions for the constraints $x_1, x_2 \sim k$ with $k = 0, 1, 2$

Some regions amount to a single point, like r0 (initial region), described by $x_1 = x_2 = 0$. Other regions are open surfaces in the plane, like the region r9, described by $0 < x_2 < x_1 < 1$, or the region r27, described by $x_1 > 2 \wedge x_2 > 1$. Lastly, the other regions are open half-lines or segments (like r7 which corresponds to $0 < x_1 = x_2 < 1$).

The system starts in the initial region r0. As time passes, the system moves on to the region r7, then on to the point $x_1 = x_2 = 1$ (r4 region), etc., and up to the r27 region. If, rather than letting time elapse, we perform a discrete transition, the resetting of certain clocks leads to regions located on the axes. For example, the reset of x_2 in region r7 leads into r8, then r9, etc.

---

[4] Contrary to hybrid systems.

Rather than analyzing the infinite configuration graph, we analyze the finite graph of the "symbolic configurations" $(q, [v])$ where $[v]$ corresponds to the region of the valuation v. This global automaton, called *region graph*, is an abstract representation of the behavior of the timed automaton. We can use this type of model to determine the truth value of the TCTL formulas.

Complexity. The number of regions grows exponentially with the number of clocks: for n clocks and for constraints in which every constant k is upper-bounded by M, the number of regions is $O(n!M^n)$. Indeed, no general and efficient method is likely to exist: whereas determining the truth value of a CTL formula on a classical automaton has linear complexity, the problem is PSPACE-complete [5] for a timed automaton and a TCTL formula [ACD93].

This explosion in the growth of the model is the major problem encountered in timed model checking. The existing tools focus on defining adequate data structures for handling the sets of regions, using for example so-called *zones*.

Regions or zones. Consider the timed automaton $\mathcal{A}$ of figure 5.6.

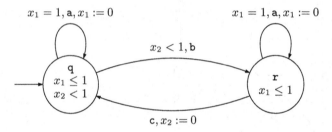

Fig. 5.6. A timed automaton

Its region graph would roughly comprise thirty states and fifty regions. In fact, some regions can be merged without adverse effects on the behavior analysis. We call *zone* a convex union of regions. Such zones were used to construct the graph $G_{\mathcal{A}}$ on figure 5.7. For example, the zone $0 \leq x_2 < x_1 < 1$ is the union of the regions $r8$ and $r9$ from figure 5.5. The states of $G_{\mathcal{A}}$ are in this case pairs (s, z) with $s \in \{q, r\}$ and z a zone.

$G_{\mathcal{A}}$ was carefully built in such a way that it corresponds to an abstraction of the behavior of $\mathcal{A}$: the executions of $G_{\mathcal{A}}$ are associated with those of $\mathcal{A}$.

---

[5] Intuitively, a problem is PSPACE-complete if it is one of the hardest among all the problems solvable using polynomial memory space. For example, the model checking of PLTL is a PSPACE-complete problem. In practice, any known algorithm will use up exponential time in the worst case. (By comparison with the more commonly known NP-completeness notion, PSPACE-complete problems do not even possess an efficient test that a purported solution discovered by chance or otherwise is indeed a solution. We refer the interested reader to the very complete book [Pap94].)

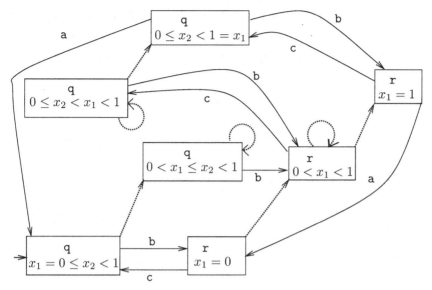

Fig. 5.7. $G_\mathcal{A}$: a symbolic representation of $\mathcal{A}$

On the one hand, for every graph label $e \in \{a, b, c\}$ in $G_\mathcal{A}$ and for every transition $(s, v) \xrightarrow{e} (s', v')$ in $\mathcal{A}$, there exists a transition $(s, z) \xrightarrow{e} (s', z')$ such that $v \in z$ et $v' \in z'$. Conversely, for every transition $(s, z) \xrightarrow{e} (s', z')$ in $\mathcal{A}$, there exists at least one clock valuation $v \in z$ such that a transition $(s, v) \xrightarrow{e} (s', v')$ with $v' \in z'$ is possible in $\mathcal{A}$. Moreover, for every transition $(s, v) \rightarrow (s, v + d)$ with $d > 0$ possible in $\mathcal{A}$ (valuations fulfilling the invariant of s), there exists a transition (dotted on the figure) $(s, z) \rightarrow (s, z')$ in $G_\mathcal{A}$.

Equipped with a labelling of the atomic propositions, the graph $G_\mathcal{A}$ can be used to decide whether $\mathcal{A}$ satisfies a CTL formula. This abstraction thus circumvents the problem of $\mathcal{A}$ possessing an infinite number of states. Checking TCTL formulas (including timed properties such as $\mathsf{EF}_{<1}P$), would require yet another abstraction (including a third clock for the purpose of measuring the formula constraints $\sim k$) but the principle of the construction would remain.

Perspectives. Timed automata are recent models. They constitute a natural formalism for the modeling of systems in which the real-time aspect is important.

In such a setting, model checking algorithms are complicated. Nevertheless, the examples presented here illustrate the general principles underlying the handling of timed systems, although some technical details were omitted and some constraints were not mentioned. For more details, we refer the reader for example to [ACD93].

The main problem lies in the complexity of the decision procedures, and in practice, what determines model checking feasibility is the number of clocks.

Existing tools (HyTech in chapter 17, Kronos in chapter 16, Uppaal in chapter 15) have nevertheless been used successfully for modeling and verifying many cases of practical interest.

Conclusion

Model checking is a verification technique that applies to a large class of systems: those which can be modeled by a finite automaton (or a variant of this general representation). It consists of three steps.

Representation of a program or a system by an automaton. Chapter 1 has shown through various examples how such a model, starting from the notions of states and transitions, can describe (part of) a system. The complete system is modeled by a new automaton, obtained by composing and synchronizing the components. The set of these components constitutes what can be termed as a network of automata. The possible behaviors of the system are modeled finally by the executions of the global automaton, the set of these executions forming a tree.

Representation of a property by a logical formula. Once the model is built, we formally state the properties to be checked, usually in a temporal logic. The logic CTL* is presented in chapter 2, as well as two particular logics derived from it. The first one, PLTL, also called linear time logic, views the system as a set of executions, while the second one, CTL, also called branching time logic, perceives the system as a tree of possible behaviors.

Model checking algorithm. Given a model $\mathcal{A}$ and a property ϕ, a model checking algorithm answers the question: "does the model $\mathcal{A}$ satisfy the property ϕ?". Chapters 3 and 4 describe the techniques employed by such algorithms in detail: explicit methods (for PLTL and CTL) and symbolic methods. Chapter 5 describes another type of model checking, dealing with a variant of the basic model: timed automata. For such models, which explicitly handle the notion of time, properties are expressed by an extension of temporal logic (TCTL). The number of states in the unfolded model here is infinite, which again entails the use of a symbolic method for model checking.

Model checking is a powerful but restricted tool:

- its power lies in the fact that it is exhaustive and automatic. A positive reply guarantees the underlying property for *all* the model behaviors. A negative reply is usually accompanied by an instructive "counter-example": a particular system execution which violates the desired property;

- its limitation is essentially due to complexity barriers: exhaustive verification, even applying symbolic methods, can prove excessively costly, in terms of time or space.

In practice, the size of systems is indeed the main obstacle yet to overcome. A system easily handled by a simulator, a compiler or an interpreter, can escape the reach of a model checker.

Model checker users are frequently forced to progressively simplify the model under analysis, until the latter is finally manageable. In this process, more and more guarantees are obtained about a model drifting further and further away from the real system. Weighing the resulting compromise is a delicate matter. Much research in progress aims at automating some aspects of this progressive simplification process, in a way that would preserve correctness. We will treat this topic in chapter 11.

Part II

Specifying with Temporal Logic

Introduction

Verification using model checking requires some expertise. Expertise alone can suggest the appropriate formulation of a problem, the way around the specific limitations of the tools at hand, and the proper interpretation of the results ultimately obtained (or lack thereof).

Acquiring this skill is a maturing process that occurs over time: hands-on experience with verification problems is required, together with some long term pondering over the model checking activity itself.

The second part of this book provides material over which to ponder. We return here to the problems encountered when constructing automata-based models and, mostly, to the writing of the temporal logic formulas expressing the desired system properties.

We aim to show how some families of properties lend themselves to particular techniques and heuristics. A prerequisite to using such techniques is of course the ability to identify their application domains. We will then be able to present the main methods used in simplifying automata, and the range of applicability of these methods.

Our starting point is a (rather classical) hierarchical classification of verification goals in terms of *reachability* properties, *safety* properties, *liveness* properties, and *fairness* properties. This classification will provide our motivation to progressively introduce both the examples and the various concepts that we wish to convey:

A *reachability property* states that some particular situation *can be reached*.

A *safety property* expresses that, under certain conditions, something *never occurs*.

A *liveness property* expresses that, under certain conditions, something *will ultimately occur*.

A *fairness property* expresses that, under certain conditions, something will (or will not) occur *infinitely often*.

L. Lamport was the first to suggest distinguishing between safety and liveness properties [Lam73]. While his motivations originated from a methodological approach, they were later backed up by theoretical work.

Distinguishing between several categories of properties is fundamental in more ways than one. From the model checking viewpoint, the following justification comes to mind:

Specification methodology. When the system set of requirements properties wish list is established, that is, when the behavioral component of the requirements is being constructed or formalized, it is worth asking the questions "which safety properties?", "which liveness properties?", etc. As a rule of thumb, this helps reducing the number of omissions and leads to specifications with a better structure.

Economy of verification. Reachability and safety properties are usually the most crucial to system correctness. Such properties therefore deserve a more substantial investment in terms of time, priority, rigor, etc., on the part of the human verifier. Luckily these properties happen in general to be the easiest ones to check.

Verification methodology. Some techniques only apply to this or that property type (see chapter 11), hence the importance of recognizing the class of a given property.

Modeling methodology. The modeling step, in principle upstream from the verification step, is in fact often tailored for specific verification goals. For example, different simplifications are called for when attempting to verify safety properties or liveness properties.

All these reasons confirm the importance of making a clear distinction between what does and does not belong to this or that family of properties. Our choice of the four families of properties listed above is in part arbitrary, and these families are not mutually exclusive. Moreover, there exist other notions (*progress* properties, *response* properties, etc.) which intersect our families to various degrees. With respect to classifying properties, the guidelines drawn from the theoretical and the practical viewpoints do not match so well. The particular choice we made was influenced by our use of temporal logic.

Chapter 11 discusses automata simplification methods. We focus on the methods that are the simplest, and the most heavily used.

The ability to pinpoint the application domain of these methods is crucial, an issue often ignored by users. We will see that the classification of properties provides a simple explanation for the preservation of some properties across this or that simplification operation.

6. Reachability Properties

A *reachability property* states that some particular situation *can be reached*.

Examples abound in practice: "we can obtain $n < 0$" (R1), "we can enter a critical section" (R2).

Often the *negation* of a reachability property is the interesting property: "we cannot have $n < 0$" (R3), "we cannot reach the `crash` state" (R4).

Reachability may be *simple*, as in the preceding examples, or *conditional*, when a condition restricts the form of the paths reaching the state involved: "we can enter the critical section without traversing $n = 0$" (R5).

Reachability may also apply *to any reachable state*. Compare "we can always return to the initial state" (R6) with "we can return to the initial state" (R7). In (R6), the *always* carries the meaning of "starting from any reachable state". Hence (R6) is a stronger property than (R7): in the latter, the ability to return to the initial state could be fulfilled in the current state and yet in no subsequent state.

6.1 Reachability in Temporal Logic

When reachability properties are expressed in temporal logic, the EF combinator appears naturally, and reachability properties can be defined as those written EFϕ, with ϕ a propositional formula free of temporal combinators (such a ϕ is often called a *present tense formula* in the temporal logic setting). Recall that EFϕ reads as "there exists a path from the current state along which some state satisfies ϕ" (see section 2.1). The examples above are formally expressed as EF$(n < 0)$ (R1), EF `crit_sec` (R2), $\neg$EF$(n < 0)$ (R3), $\neg$EF `crash` (R4). Recall that by duality $\neg$EFϕ can also be expressed as AG$\neg\phi$ (which reads as "along every path, at any time, $\neg\phi$").

Reachability from any reachable state requires nesting the AG and EF combinators: (R6) is expressed as AG(EF `init`).

Conditional reachability naturally uses the E_U_ construct, where the U (*until*) replaces the F. (R5) is written E$(n \neq 0)$U `crit_sec`, which reads as "there exists a path along which $n \neq 0$ holds until `crit_sec` becomes true".

All the previous examples use the logic CTL. We note that the linear temporal logic PLTL is poorly suited for reachability properties. Insofar, as it implicitly quantifies over all executions, PLTL can only express reachability negatively: something is not reachable. Nested reachability is not expressible in PLTL (see section 2.4).

6.2 Model Checkers and Reachability

Reachability properties are typically the easiest to verify.

When a model checking tool is able to construct the reachability graph of a system, it can *in principle* answer any reachability question by simply examining this graph, even if it does not include temporal logic.

All the tools described in the third part of this book can answer reachability questions in one form or another, and we consider such capabilities as constituting the minimal functionalities of any model checker.

But these functionalities do vary in richness: some tools allow one to constrain the executions (for conditional reachability), or choosing an arbitrary set of starting states (for nested reachability), or verifying the reachability of a family of states (for example "all the states in which $n = 0$").

Some tools, for example DESIGN/CPN (see chapter 14), are specifically designed for the verification of reachability properties, and they offer numerous options aimed at helping the user circumvent the state explosion problem. For example, DESIGN/CPN performs partial construction of the state graph, under control of the user who may explicitly specify which parts of the graph may be pruned away.

6.3 Computation of the Reachability Graph

The set of reachable states is in general not immediately apparent from a simple look at the system. Whenever several automata are synchronized (or when variables, clocks, counters, etc., are used) the effective construction of the set of reachable states becomes non-trivial.

Two large families of algorithms deal with reachability problems: "forward chaining" algorithms and "backward chaining" algorithms.

Forward chaining. This is the natural approach which comes to mind: to build the set of reachable states, we start from the initial states, we add their successors, and we go on until saturation, that is, until no new state gets added to the set. The way to compute the immediate successors depends on the type of automaton under consideration but it is generally simple, being in fact the job of any simulation tool.

The only difficulty is practical: it is the potential explosion of the size of the set being constructed.

Backward chaining. Here the idea is to construct the set of states which can lead to some target states (that is, to the states whose reachability is in question): we start from these target states, we add their immediate predecessors, and we continue until saturation. We then test whether some initial state is in the resulting saturated set. This procedure is nothing but the enumerative version of the $Pre^*(S)$ algorithm from section 4.1.

Backward search has two drawbacks as compared to forward search. First, a set of target states needs to be fixed before the backward search can even begin: one cannot *a priori* construct the reachability graph and then check whether this or that state appears. Note that this hindrance nonetheless carries a positive aspect: the target states are an additional parameter to play with in the process of controlling the verification.

Second, computing the immediate predecessors is generally more complicated than computing the successors. This of course depends on the model: for example, in the case of automata rigged with variables and guarded transitions and intricate assignments, the immediate successors are much more easily obtained (it suffices to evaluate expressions) than the immediate predecessors (these require solving equations and finding which values of the variables yield the appropriate expression evaluation).

In the end, the two approaches are complementary. To find out whether a set S is reachable, one can in the forward manner compute the reachability set and check whether it intersects S, or one can compute $Pre^*(S)$ and check whether this intersects the set of initial states.

It often happens that one approach terminates rapidly and the other stalls, victim of the state explosion problem. Such situations can be baffling because one can most often not predict which approach is more likely to succeed. To see why, imagine an unreachable target set S. In that case, the sets encountered by both algorithms are totally disjoint from one another, and the size of one set offers no clue as to the size of the other.

"On-the-fly" exploration. To answer reachability questions, "on-the-fly" methods *explore* the reachability graph without actually building it. The aim is still to construct the graph, but this construction is only performed partially, as the exploration proceeds, and without remembering everything that was already visited. This approach tries to exploit the fact that present-day computers are more limited in their memory resource than they are in their processing speed.

From a practical point of view, the reader should remember the following: on-the-fly methods are efficient mostly when the target set is indeed reachable (the "yes" answer does not require an exhaustive exploration); they can operate in the forward or in the backward manner, even though they have traditionally been applied in the former manner; finally, they may also apply to some systems with infinitely many states.

7. Safety Properties

A *safety property* expresses that, under certain conditions, an event *never occurs*.

Examples are everywhere, most often without conditions: "both processes will never be in their critical section simultaneously [1]" (S1), or "memory overflow will never occur" (S2), or "the situation ... is impossible" (S3). An example of safety with condition is "as long as the key is not in the ignition position, the car won't start" (S4).

In general, and as can be seen from these examples, safety statements express that an undesirable event will not occur, hence the "safety property" terminology.

The same examples show that the negation of a reachability property is a safety property (compare (A3) and (S3)), and that the negation of a safety property is a reachability property.

7.1 Safety Properties in Temporal Logic

Combinators AG in CTL, G in PLTL express safety properties in the most natural way.

In CTL, we can state (S1) and (S2) by e.g. $AG\neg(crit\_sec_1 \land crit\_sec_2)$ and $AG\neg overflow$. The corresponding formulations in PLTL (that is, respectively, $G\neg(crit\_sec_1 \land crit\_sec_2)$ and $G\neg overflow$) are equivalent [2].

Numerous safety properties with attached conditions, for example "as long as the key is not in the ignition position, the car won't start" (S4), are expressed naturally with the W combinator (the *weak until*). (S4) is expressed formally by:

$$A\neg starts \; W \; key \qquad\qquad (7.1)$$

---

[1] The archetype of a mutual exclusion property.

[2] Here, when we say that ϕ and ψ are "equivalent" , we mean that they express the same property *on automata*: $\mathcal{A} \models \phi$ if and only if $\mathcal{A} \models \psi$. Therefore, this is not the formal notion of logical equivalence, denoted $\equiv$ and used elsewhere. For example we cannot replace ϕ by ψ within a more complicated formula.

which reads literally as "whatever the behavior (A) is, the car never starts (¬starts) unless (W) the key is inserted into the ignition (key)". In PLTL, ¬starts W key is an equivalent transcription of (7.1).

An expression using the strong *until*:

$$A¬starts \, U \, key \tag{7.2}$$

does not faithfully correspond to (S4). The difference between (7.1) and (7.2) is due to the difference between U and W: the strong *until* requires that we will some day end up having key. Consequently, and as we will explain in section 8.1, the property (7.2) is not a safety property.

7.2 A Formal Definition

The definition of safety properties given at the beginning of chapter 7 was informal and thus ambiguous. Our reasons to underline the importance of the notion of a safety property require that we provide a more precise definition.

It is rather tricky to give such a definition *in a general sense*. Propositions can be found in the literature [LS85, ADS86, AS87, Kin94]. These all arise from the informal idea that *the fewer things we do, the more chances we have that a safety property be verified*. In other words, the only way to satisfy all the safety properties is to stay put and do nothing! A "topological" notion of a safety property thus follows: it is any property P such that if a behavior C satisfies P then any reduced behavior $C' \sqsubseteq C$ *a fortiori* satisfies P. Of course, we should now provide a formal definition of what constitutes a reduced behavior with respect to another. For example, for the sets of executions C and C', we can define $C' \sqsubseteq C$ by "any execution in C' is the prefix of an execution in C". Another possibility is offered by the notion of "simulation" between execution trees [Mil89].

Syntactic characterization. In the particular case of a P expressed in temporal logic, we can provide syntactic characterizations [Sis85, MP90, CMP92, Sis94]. An elegant one states that any safety property can be written in the form $AG\phi^-$ where ϕ^- is a *past* temporal formula, that is, using only past combinators (see below) together with the usual boolean combinators and atomic propositions. The formulation $G\phi^-$, for PLTL, is equivalent.

The principle underlying this characterization is the following: when a safety property is violated, it should be possible to instantly notice it. If this depends on the remainder of the behavior, then a behavior which would end immediately would not violate the safety property. Hence we can only notice it, in the current state, relying on events which occurred earlier (in a loose sense: here the past includes the present).

Temporal logic with past. The logic CTL* does not provide past combinators. This does not prevent CTL* from expressing safety properties. It only precludes giving such a simple and elegant characterization of the notion of a safety property.

Without giving a formal definition (see [LS95] for this), past temporal combinators can be described as those that are a mirror image of future combinators. In this way $F^{-1}\phi$ and $X^{-1}\phi$ mean that ϕ was verified at some past instant (for F^{-1}), or in the state immediately preceding the present instant (for X^{-1}). The S operator is the mirror of *until*, U. The formula $\phi S \psi$ means that ψ was fulfilled at a past instant, and that, since then, ϕ is fulfilled.

The one very subtle point in past temporal logic lies in the interpretation of formulas *on the tree of possible behaviors*. Thus $F^{-1}\phi$ does not refer to an ancestor state in the graph, but to a state encountered along the initial portion of the execution leading to the state in which we find ourselves now. This is why we do not use the path combinators A and E together with past combinators: the past of the current state is fixed, it is the path which led from the initial state to the current state.

$AG\phi^-$ in practice. Mutual exclusion, which can be written $AG\neg(sc_1 \wedge sc_2)$, is indeed a safety formula: the sub-formula $\neg(sc_1 \wedge sc_2)$ in which no future combinator occurs is a potential ϕ^-.

Let us return to the example of the property (7.1). It can be written in the form:

$$AG(\texttt{starts} \Rightarrow F^{-1}\texttt{key}) \tag{7.3}$$

which only uses past combinators (here F^{-1}) within the scope of the AG. This formula reads as "it is always true (AG) that if the car starts, then ($\Rightarrow$) the key was inserted beforehand (F^{-1})". It therefore is a safety property indeed!

The characterization of safety properties in the form $AG\phi^-$ makes it clear that if ψ_1 and ψ_2 are safety formulas, then their conjunction $\psi_1 \wedge \psi_2$ is again a safety formula, whereas their disjunction is in general not. For example, $(AGP) \vee (AGQ)$ is equivalent to no formula $AG\phi^-$.

Safety properties and diagnostic. The characterization in the form $AG\phi^-$ helps to explain the form of the diagnostics provided by model checkers in response to a safety formula that is not satisfied.

If a property $AG\phi^-$ is not satisfied, then there necessarily exists a *finite* path leading from the initial state to the undesirable situation. Such an execution prefix is a sufficient diagnostic. It embodies all the information required to observe that ϕ^- is not fulfilled: since ϕ^- is a past formula, it is not necessary to know how the execution (which is probably infinite) would carry on further.

For the same reason, even if a safety property is not given in an explicit past form, a consequence of the characterization by $AG\phi^-$ is that there always exists a finite execution prefix sufficient for diagnostic purposes (when the property is violated).

7.3 Safety Properties in Practice

In an ideal situation, a safety property is verified simply by submitting it to a model checker. In real life, hurdles spring up.

In this section, we tour some of the practical problems encountered when verifying safety properties, and we use these problems as a motivation to describe specific methods. So called abstraction methods lie in a specific class and are described in chapter 11. For the moment, note simply that abstraction methods target the *state explosion or system size* problem, and that abstraction methods can be used in combination with the other methods.

We proceed from the simplest to the most complicated situation.

A simple case: non-reachability. In practice, a large number of safety properties are expressed as outright negated reachability properties: "the system cannot reach a state in which ...".

We are thus faced with a $\neg\mathsf{EF}(\ldots)$, that is, with a $\mathsf{AG}\phi^-$ where ϕ^- is a local property, for example $\neg(\mathtt{crit\_in}_1 \wedge \mathtt{crit\_in}_2)$, that is, with a formula free of past or future temporal combinators, also called *present formula*.

This is a very important and frequent special case. In principle, it is one of the simplest cases, for which everything presented in chapter 6 applies.

Safety without past. Very often, a safety property is given in a form not using the past. For example, $\mathsf{A}(\neg\mathtt{starts}\ \mathsf{W}\ \mathtt{key})$ (7.1) is encountered more often than $\mathsf{AG}(\mathtt{starts} \Rightarrow \mathsf{F}^{-1}\mathtt{key})$ (7.3) in formal specifications.

Which to go for, (7.1) or (7.3)? The former appears more natural to most model checker users. This owes to the fact that no model checker is currently able to deal with past formulas, so that almost all presentations (and especially all practical uses) of temporal logic rely on logics of the future. Chapter 2 here was no exception.

However, note two advantages in using mixed logic:

- mixed logic allows one to write formulas $\mathsf{AG}\phi^-$ with a syntax that guarantees that these are safety formulas. Such guarantees are less obvious in future logic, suffice it to compare (7.1) with (7.2), where only the former formula is a safety property;
- mixed logic provides a richer formalism, better suited to the transcription of natural language statements which tend to mix past and future adverbs freely.

For safety formulas without past, the first problem is therefore their identification. Once identified, such formulas can be dealt with directly if the model checker at our disposal handles temporal logic. Otherwise, we can use the method of history variables, described in section 7.4.

Safety with explicit past. Recall that at present (to the best of our knowledge) no model checker is able to handle temporal formulas with past. To deal with a safety property of the form $\mathsf{AG}\phi^-$, two approaches are possible: the *eliminating the past*, which we describe briefly, and the *history variables method*, which we will consider in the next section.

Eliminating the past. In principle, it is possible to translate any temporal logic formula combining past and future into an equivalent pure-future formula [LS95]. Note that, in the case of a formula $AG\phi^-$, the result is not necessarily a CTL formula. These translations however turn out to be rather delicate and, in practice, the fall-back position is to rely on several simple schemas, such as $AG(\ldots \Rightarrow F^{-1}\ldots)$ for which the equivalent is given once and for all:

$$AG(\phi \Rightarrow F^{-1}\psi) \;\equiv\; A(\neg\phi W\psi).$$

7.4 The History Variables Method

It is possible in practice to reduce handling a property of the form $AG\phi^-$ to handling a reachability property. This is a rather simple procedure and, in any case, it is the only available course of action when the tool at our disposal is unable to deal with temporal logic. We thus see that, depending on the available tool, a formulation with explicit past may have its advantages.

The method to translate a formula $AG\phi^-$ into a reachability property hinges on the use of *history variables*. The purpose of a history variable is to store the occurrences of some (past) events without modifying the (future) behavior of the system. Such history variables can then be used in reachability formulas to express $AG\phi^-$.

An example. The construction can be illustrated on a simple example. Consider the automaton $\mathcal{A}$ in figure 7.1.

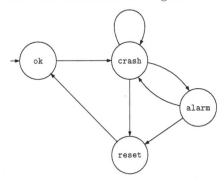

Fig. 7.1. $\mathcal{A}$, a model of an alarm

We wish to check that every time the **alarm** goes off, a **crash** has necessarily occurred beforehand, which is expressible as $AG(\text{alarm} \Rightarrow F^{-1}\text{crash})$ using the F^{-1} combinator ("there happened in the past"). Moreover, we wish to verify that every time the **alarm** goes off, no **reset** had occurred since the last **crash**. The combination of these two properties can be expressed with the help of the S combinator: $\mathsf{AG}\,(\texttt{alarm} \Rightarrow (\neg\textbf{reset})S\,\textbf{crash})$.

We also wish to verify that every sounding of the **alarm** was immediately preceded by a **crash**, which is expressed simply as $\mathsf{AG}\,(\texttt{alarm} \Rightarrow \mathsf{X}^{-1}\textbf{crash})$ with the X^{-1} combinator (for "the immediate predecessor state"). These three properties are of the form $\mathsf{AG}\phi^-$ and are thus safety properties.

It is possible to get rid of past formulas ϕ^- by introducing history variables. For a formula ϕ^-, a history variable is a boolean variable $\mathbf{h}_{\phi^-}$ which holds **true** if and only if ϕ^- is true. Since ϕ^- is a past formula, it is possible to update the history variable $\mathbf{h}_{\phi^-}$ upon each transition, without having to know what the remainder of the behavior will be.

In the example above, we need two variables: **h1** for the formula $\mathsf{X}^{-1}\textbf{crash}$ (referred to as ϕ_1^-) and **h2** for $(\neg\textbf{reset})S\,\textbf{crash}$ (referred to as ϕ_2^-). We will modify the automaton of figure 7.1 to incorporate **h1** and **h2**, which must correctly represent the values of ϕ_1^- and ϕ_2^-.

For $\mathsf{X}^{-1}\textbf{crash}$, the update is easy: **h1** is initially **false**. Then, a transition from q to q' assigns **true** to **h1** if and only if q satisfies **crash**, that is if q is the **crash** state.

For **h2**, the strategy is similar. Here ϕ_2^- is $(\neg\textbf{reset})S\,\textbf{crash}$. We set **h2** to **false** initially. Then each transition landing into the **crash** state sets **h2** to **true**. The other transitions set **h2** to **false** if they land into the **reset** state, leaving the variable unchanged otherwise. This leads to the automaton on figure 7.2.

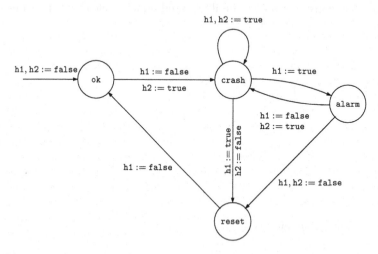

Fig. 7.2. $\mathcal{A}_{+\text{hist}}$, the automaton $\mathcal{A}$ enriched with its history variables

The resulting automaton, $\mathcal{A}_{+\text{hist}}$, has the same behavior as $\mathcal{A}$ (and it thus satisfies the same temporal logic formulas) but the two additional variables are such that:

AG ($\text{h1} \Leftrightarrow \text{X}^{-1}\text{crash}$) and AG ($\text{h2} \Leftrightarrow (\neg\text{reset})\text{S crash}$).

We thus reduce a question of the form "does $\mathcal{A} \models$ AG ($\text{alarm} \Rightarrow \text{X}^{-1}\text{crash}$)?" to a model checking problem without past "does $\mathcal{A}_{+\text{hist}} \models$ AG ($\text{alarm} \Rightarrow \text{h1}$)?" handled directly by tools like SMV.

The general case. The construction suggested above applies in general. It suffices to introduce one history variable for each sub-formula having at its root a past combinator. Consider for example the formula $\text{F}^{-1}((\text{X}^{-1}P)\text{S}Q)$, we introduce h1 for $\text{X}^{-1}P$, then h2 for h1 S Q, then h3 for F^{-1}h2. These three variables are initially false and they are updated using the technique illustrated on the example of figure 7.2, remembering that F^{-1} is a special case of S and that G^{-1} is dual to F^{-1}.

Note that the history variables method always leads to (the negation of) a reachability problem. Thus the technique proves useful to model-check safety formulas without past when the tool at our disposal only handles reachability.

More generally, the history variables method can be viewed as a special (and simplified) case of the observer automata method. By comparison with this second method, the great advantage of history variables is that in practice, the modifications required are both easy to understand and easy to justify.

Complexity. Since the introduction of each boolean variable doubles the number of states in the unfolded automaton, the history variables method can lead to combinatorial explosion if the size of the past formulas is not kept in check. Accordingly, model checking for CTL enriched with past combinators is PSPACE-complete.

8. Liveness Properties

A *liveness property* states that, under certain conditions, some event *will ultimately occur.*

Examples abound: "any request will ultimately be satisfied" (L1), or "by keeping on trying, one will eventually succeed" (L2), or "if we call on the elevator, it is bound to arrive eventually" (L3), or "the light will turn green" (L4), or finally "after the rain, the sunshine" (L5).

Note that mere reachability is not the issue: (L4) states that the light will turn green (some day) regardless of the system behavior, which demands a lot more than the plain reachability property "it is possible for the light (some day) to turn green".

As the rather positive *liveness* terminology suggests, the general meaning of a liveness property is to state that some *happy* event will occur in the end. This is the case with the previous examples but, of course, the subjective aspect is not part of the definition.

Surprisingly, "the program will terminate" (L6) is a liveness property. This example is all the more paradoxical that some confusion sometimes exists between liveness properties (the topic of this chapter) and *the* liveness, that is, "the property of being live". In many settings, the property of being live means that each system component remains reachable ("firable" in the case of a transition) indefinitely.

A formal definition. It is not easy to formally capture the notion of a liveness property. Some definitions have been proposed in the literature [AS85, AS87, Kin94] but, in our opinion, their interest is essentially theoretical. For example these definitions support variants of the so-called decomposition theorem, stating that any arbitrary property is the conjunction (the $\wedge$) of a safety property and a liveness property [AS85]. This theorem forms the theoretical basis for the methodological advice given in the introduction to the second part of this book.

Now if our goal is to syntactically characterize the temporal logic formulas that express liveness properties, the scientific literature offers suggestions that are more interesting in practice, but suffer from another disadvantage: they break up the set of liveness properties into a significant number of distinct subclasses: progress properties, response properties, etc. [Sis85, CMP92, Sis94].

We only mention here that there exist two broad families of liveness properties: simple liveness, which we may call *progress*, and repeated liveness, which is sometimes called *fairness*. Interest in this distinction is essentially due to the specification methodology.

The rest of this chapter is devoted to simple liveness, and we postpone our treatment of fairness properties until chapter 10.

8.1 Simple Liveness in Temporal Logic

The F combinator is the one that expresses liveness in the most transparent way. Consider some examples:

- "any request will ultimately be satisfied" is expressed as $\mathsf{AG}(\mathtt{req} \Rightarrow \mathsf{AF}\,\mathtt{sat})$ in CTL and as $\mathsf{G}(\mathtt{req} \Rightarrow \mathsf{F}\,\mathtt{sat})$ in PLTL.
- "The system can always return to its initial state" is expressed as $\mathsf{AGEF}\,\mathtt{init}$ in CTL. (In PLTL, no direct formulation of this notion exists, so that we can only express it if we have an explicit characterization of the set of states satisfying $\mathsf{EF}\,\mathtt{init}$.)

The U combinator is more complicated. Recall that $P\mathsf{U}Q$ means that, along the current execution, we will find a state satisfying Q and P will hold for all the states encountered in the meantime.

Here, the guarantee that Q will eventually hold clearly is a liveness property. Moreover, the constraint that P will always hold beforehand is a safety property.

Thus $P\mathsf{W}Q$ (where we do not require that a state satisfying Q exists) is a safety property and $P\mathsf{U}Q$, which combines safety and liveness aspects, is classified, for lack of a better alternative, as a liveness property. The equivalence

$$P\mathsf{U}Q \;\equiv\; \mathsf{F}Q \wedge (P\mathsf{W}Q)$$

is an instance of the decomposition theorem mentioned to at the beginning of this chapter.

If we use CTL combinators, $\mathsf{A}P\mathsf{U}Q$ and $\mathsf{E}P\mathsf{U}Q$ are liveness properties. (The strong *until* is required: with W, the formula $\mathsf{A}P\mathsf{W}Q$ is a safety property.)

8.2 Are Liveness Properties Useful?

Some authors claim that for the practical purpose of verification, the only useful properties are safety properties. They argue that a liveness property only guarantees that an event will occur "some day" without giving a hint as to the delays involved. What good is proving that "if we call on the elevator, it is bound to arrive eventually" if we cannot tell that it will arrive within a bounded and reasonable time delay? From a utilitarian viewpoint, the liveness property yields no information. We speak of an "abstract" liveness property. Now if we strengthen the property to a "bounded" liveness property (that is, to a property of the form "an event will occur within at most x time units", see section 8.5), then we obtain a safety property, and this supports these authors' claim.

Without brushing off these objections, it is nonetheless possible to justify the interest in stating and/or verifying that a system fulfills abstract liveness properties. For the theoretician, the interest is in being able to express things at a high level of abstraction and generality. For the practitioner, the interest is in the added simplicity and efficiency. The arguments in favor of abstract liveness properties are divided into three broad categories:

"Abstract" more general than "concrete". Requirements identify goals without pinning down the implementation details. In some cases, bounded liveness violates this abstraction principle.

A clear example is provided by parametrized systems, that is, whose final structure depends on a parameter which may vary, for example an n-story elevator, or a network of n computers. The bounded liveness properties depend (sometimes in complicated ways) on the value of the parameter whereas the abstract liveness is an abstract goal independent of this value.

More generally, the model submitted to a model checker does not account for all the details of the real system being modeled. In some cases, a bounded liveness property of the real system is not expressible in terms of the bounded liveness of the model.

"Abstract" more efficient than "concrete". An abstract liveness property is simpler to write and to read than a bounded liveness property.

Next, bounded liveness necessarily refers to a timed behavior of the system, which cannot always be modeled by the tools at hand, and which in any case always involves a very high cost in terms of complexity. In practice, it is much simpler to verify an abstract liveness property than a bounded liveness property.

"Abstract" and "concrete" are not contradictory. Of course, if the abstract liveness property is not fulfilled, any bounded variant of the same property is *a fortiori* not satisfied.

In the opposite direction, for a given model, in principle we can extract bounds on the liveness *a posteriori* from a proof that the model verifies the abstract liveness property. Also, the abstract liveness property is often present during certain steps of the formalization, and it is only later made precise in the form of a bounded liveness property. It is important to be able to relate these two versions of liveness.

Liveness properties thus remain a precious tool, indispensable in some cases. The objections raised at the beginning of this chapter nonetheless support our position from chapter 7, namely that more time and rigor should be devoted to the verification of safety properties.

8.3 Liveness in the Model, Liveness in the Properties

By comparison with the simpler reachability and safety properties, liveness properties can play two rather different roles in the verification process. They can indeed either appear as liveness *properties* that we wish to verify, or as liveness *hypotheses* that we make on the system model.

In this section we will first investigate the liveness hypotheses which implicitly occur in the models. Then we will explain why these hypotheses are not always those that are sought, and how it can be difficult, if not impossible, to impose some liveness properties to a given family of models. We will then show how it is possible with model checking to add these hypotheses from outside the system. We will come across a similar situation later on when studying fairness properties (chapter 10).

Implicit hypotheses. When we use a mathematical model (for example automata) to represent a real system, the semantics of the model in fact define *implicit safety and liveness hypotheses*.

The safety hypotheses are obvious: the automaton can flip from state q to state q' only if it includes a transition going from q to q'. Even though these hypotheses are implicit, they are so natural that their non-explanation causes no misunderstanding.

Such is not the case with the liveness hypotheses. In the case of an automaton, the implicit hypothesis made is that the system will chain transitions as long as possible. Thus a system execution can only be finite if it leads to a blocked state (state with no successor). Note that this hypothesis pertains to the states (or to the sets of transitions originating from a state), not to the transitions themselves.

A variant of this model includes *accepting states*. The liveness hypothesis then allows (and requires) terminating in such a state.

In any case, the hypothesis is that the system does not terminate without reason, or that it does not remain inactive indefinitely without reason.

In the case of timed systems (see chapter 5), some models assume that all transitions are urgent (they occur as soon as possible) and they wait only if they must synchronize with another component.

The liveness hypotheses underlying a model (the *implicit* hypotheses) can be subtle and can cause errors. The model may seem to reproduce certain aspects of the real system faithfully, when its behavior is actually different.

Consider for example the automaton on figure 8.1 (reproduced from chapter 1).

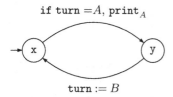

Fig. 8.1. The user A

This is a system that wishes to print (in state x) but can proceed only if turn $= A$ (turn is a global variable that other components can modify). If turn $\neq A$, the system must wait. When turn $= A$, the system can print and enter state y. In state y the system ends up returning to state x, assigning B to turn in the process.

Thus the system modeled by figure 8.1, when in state x, will always end up wishing to print (since this is the only possible behavior)! A real "user A" does not necessarily operate in this way, and perhaps this slight difference between the model and the real system results from an oversight. Perhaps adding a self-loop transition from x to x would yield a model more faithful to the reality. (In the same way, in state y, the model will end up entering state x. Here the hypothesis is justifiable on the grounds that it serves to require that the printing operation always terminate.)

The difficulties just raised are inherent to the modeling activity: one must be aware of the premises of the models used and check their adequacy. Sometimes it is not possible to incorporate the liveness hypotheses which seem necessary into a given model.

A well-known case is that of networks of automata operating in parallel. If we combine two automata $\mathcal{A}_1$ and $\mathcal{A}_2$ by asynchronous parallelism, the resulting system is an automaton with global liveness hypotheses: in $\mathcal{A}_1 \parallel \mathcal{A}_2$ it is not possible to stay put indefinitely, but we tolerate that one of the components should remain inactive indefinitely! Thus, liveness properties of individual components are not preserved by a synchronized product.

Figure 8.2 gives a simple example. In the automaton $\mathcal{A}_1$, Q is unavoidable ($\mathcal{A}_1 \models \mathsf{AF}Q$). It can even be stated that Q will unavoidably occur infinitely often ($\mathcal{A}_1 \models \mathsf{A}\overset{\infty}{\mathsf{F}}\,Q$). However it suffices to compose $\mathcal{A}_1$ asynchronously with another automaton $\mathcal{A}_2$, that is to put them side by side, and this property is no longer ensured by the model.

Let us make clear that this problem cannot be solved by "correcting" the definition of the synchronization operation. It is the finite automaton model which must be upgraded (for example by the introduction in the automata of repeated states *à la* Büchi), and this in general is not possible when we are tied to the model underlying a specific model checker.

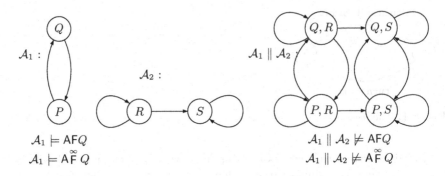

Fig. 8.2. The liveness of $\mathcal{A}_1$ does not carry over to $\mathcal{A}_1 \parallel \mathcal{A}_2$

8.4 Verification under Liveness Hypotheses

In the case where a mismatch exists between the real system behavior and the liveness hypotheses made by the model, verification by model checking remains possible if two conditions are met:

- the liveness hypotheses of the model must be less constraining than the desired liveness hypothesis: the behaviors of the model are more general than those of the real system. The example of figure 8.2 fulfills this requirement. We would wish liveness of the product $\mathcal{A}_1 \parallel \mathcal{A}_2$ to combine the liveness of $\mathcal{A}_1$ and $\mathcal{A}_2$. In fact more general behaviors are possible in $\mathcal{A}_1 \parallel \mathcal{A}_2$: those where one of the components is completely ignored;
- the temporal logic must be rich enough to express the liveness hypotheses that are not guaranteed by the model. For instance, CTL and PLTL handle simple liveness. For repeated liveness, CTL+fairness (see chapter 10) or PLTL are required.

In this case we wish to verify that *specific model behaviors* (that is, only those for which the liveness hypothesis hold, say ϕ_v) satisfy a given property (say ψ). Also, by assumption, we can express in temporal logic the behaviors that verify the liveness hypothesis, for example all the paths satisfying ϕ_v.

It then suffices to verify $\phi_v \Rightarrow \psi$ on the model at our disposal. This formula states that ψ holds for the behaviors of interest.

In general, ϕ_v is a property pertaining to the executions. It can therefore naturally be written in PLTL. If ψ is also a PLTL formula then the formula $\phi_v \Rightarrow \psi$ will be a PLTL formula and we will check $\phi_v \Rightarrow \psi$ as we would have done for ψ.

If ψ is written in CTL, then we will have to insert the hypothesis ϕ_v on each occurrence of a quantifier A or E in ψ. For example AF EPUQ will lead to:

$$\mathsf{A}\left(\phi_v \Rightarrow \mathsf{F}\,\mathsf{E}(\phi_v \wedge PUQ)\right).$$

The result in general becomes a CTL* formula but if ϕ_v is sufficiently simple, CTL equivalents exist. For example, if ϕ_v is a PLTL formula with no nested temporal combinators, then "ψ under hypothesis ϕ_v" can be written in CTL [1].

8.5 Bounded Liveness

A bounded liveness property is a liveness property that comes with a maximal delay within which the "desired situation" must occur. For example, we can require that "any request be satisfied *within less than 15 days*", or that "the light turn green *within 3 minutes*".

From a theoretical viewpoint, *these properties are safety properties!*

We can explain this paradox: suppose that our bounded liveness property is of the general form "ψ_1 will necessarily occur before (or at the latest when) ψ_2". If this property is not fulfilled along an execution, it is because some day ψ_2 holds and ψ_1 was never satisfied beforehand. Our bounded liveness property can thus be written in the form $\mathsf{AG}(\psi_2 \Rightarrow \mathsf{F}^{-1}\psi_1)$, which is indeed a safety property of the form $\mathsf{AG}\phi^-$ if ψ_1 et ψ_2 do not involve temporal operators.

Note that this remark applies in general, without the "bound" ψ_2 necessarily referencing concrete measures of time: clock values, numbers of transitions already performed, etc.

A happy consequence is that all the techniques seen in chapter 7 and tied to the verification of safety properties easily apply to bounded liveness properties.

Nonetheless, from a methodological viewpoint, bounded liveness properties are not as important as true safety properties. We thus maintain our recommendation to devote less efforts to their verification.

Bounded liveness in timed systems. Bounded liveness properties are most often encountered in the specification of timed systems (see chapter 5). Indeed, in such situations it is possible to express and to verify explicit constraints on the delays.

Consider for example the following properties: "the program terminates in less than ten seconds" (BL1), or "any request is satisfied in less than five minutes" (BL2).

Using a notation inspired by TCTL (see chapter 5), (BL1) can be expressed formally as $\mathsf{AF}_{<10s}\mathsf{end}$ and (BL2) as $\mathsf{AG}(\mathsf{req} \Rightarrow \mathsf{AF}_{<5m}\mathsf{sat})$.

All these formulas are in fact safety properties that can be written in the form $\mathsf{AG}\phi^-$. For example, (BL1) can be written $\mathsf{AG}(\neg\mathsf{end} \Rightarrow \mathsf{F}^{-1}_{<10s}\mathsf{start})$. An equivalent formulation for (BL2) is $\mathsf{AG}(\neg(\mathsf{F}^{-1}_{=5m}\mathsf{req} \wedge \mathsf{G}^{-1}_{\leq5m}\neg\mathsf{sat}))$.

This feature of timed models partly explains the lack of functionalities allows one to verify liveness properties in tools like UPPAAL (see chapter 15)

---

[1] See the translation of the CTL$^+$ formulas into CTL formulas given in [Eme90].

and HYTECH (see chapter 17). Today KRONOS is the only model checker for timed systems in which liveness properties (described in TCTL) can be checked.

9. Deadlock-freeness

Deadlock-freeness is a special property, stating that the system can never be in a situation in which no progress is possible. This is a correctness property relevant for systems that are supposed to run indefinitely. In a more general framework, a set of properly identified final states will be required to be deadlock-free.

Deadlock-freeness is a very important property in many cases. It does fit the general pattern "some undesirable event will never occur" and one is tempted to declare it a safety property. This is indeed the way that the property is treated by many authors.

9.1 Safety? Liveness?

In full generality, deadlock-freeness is written $\mathsf{AG\,EX\,true}$ in CTL, which reads as "whatever the state reached may be (AG), there will exist an immediate successor state ($\mathsf{EX\,true}$)".

This statement is not of the form $\mathsf{AG}\phi^-$. At first glance, it does not seem possible to come up with an equivalent formulation of the form $\mathsf{AG}\phi^-$. Actually, from a theoretical viewpoint, *deadlock-freeness is not a safety property*.

We will return to this point in the following sections. For the moment, we stress the important issues in practice:

1. Deadlock-freeness can be verified if the model checker at our disposal can handle $\mathsf{AG\,EX\,true}$ (for example a model checker for CTL).
2. Moreover, it may be incorrect to prove deadlock-freeness by relying on methods tied to safety properties (see chapter 11).
3. When the tool at our disposal cannot handle $\mathsf{AG\,EX\,true}$, we can try to directly express deadlock-freeness with respect to the automaton being investigated.

9.2 Deadlock-freeness for a Given Automaton

We sometimes think of deadlock-freeness as a safety property because, *for a given automaton*, we can often describe the deadlocked states explicitly. It then suffices to verify that they cannot be reached.

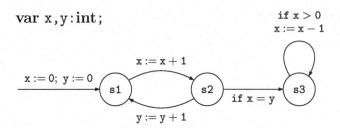

Fig. 9.1. $\mathcal{A}$: A deadlock-free system

Consider the example $\mathcal{A}$ on figure 9.1. There we have a simple automaton with two integer variables. The two rightmost transitions are guarded by conditions on the variable values. The automaton is deadlock-free because the x and y values are always equal in state s1, and always different in state s2, so that state s3 can never be reached.

For that system, the deadlocked states are those in which the control state is s3 and in which x is less than or equal to zero. Thus, instead of using AG EX true, we can express the deadlock-freeness of this model by:

$$\mathcal{A} \models \mathsf{AG}\neg(\mathsf{s3} \wedge \mathsf{x} \leq 0) \tag{9.1}$$

and the formula (9.1) is indeed a safety property (it has the form $\mathsf{AG}\phi^-$).

Let us point out that (9.1) expresses deadlock-freeness only for the automaton on figure 9.1. Now consider $\mathcal{A}'$, a variant of $\mathcal{A}$ obtained by forbidding the transition from s2 to s1 (see figure 9.2).

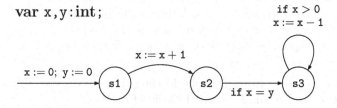

Fig. 9.2. $\mathcal{A}'$: A variant of the previous example

The behaviors of $\mathcal{A}'$ form a subset of the behaviors of $\mathcal{A}$ (because some transitions were removed) and, consequently, all the safety properties satisfied by $\mathcal{A}$ also hold for $\mathcal{A}'$. Actually, $\mathcal{A}'$ satisfies (9.1)! However $\mathcal{A}'$ is not deadlock-free: once the state s2 is reached, the system is deadlocked, so that (9.1) no longer expresses deadlock-freeness.

9.3 Beware of Abstractions!

A dual phenomenon occurs if we add transitions: even if the system we obtain is deadlock-free, this does not guarantee that the initial system was (as would be the case for a safety property). Consider $\mathcal{A}''$, a variant of $\mathcal{A}'$ obtained by abstracting away the internal variables (see figure 9.3).

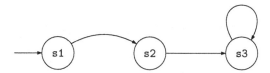

Fig. 9.3. $\mathcal{A}''$: An abstraction of $\mathcal{A}'$

The behaviors of $\mathcal{A}''$ are less restricted than those of $\mathcal{A}'$ since there are no more guards to forbid transitions. (Without variables, $\mathcal{A}''$ does not require unfolding, it only has three states and is trivially deadlock-free.)

The abstraction operation performed when going from $\mathcal{A}'$ to $\mathcal{A}''$ is compatible with safety properties, nevertheless the fact that $\mathcal{A}''$ is deadlock-free does not prove that $\mathcal{A}'$ is.

10. Fairness Properties

A *fairness property* expresses that, under certain conditions, an event will occur (or will fail to occur) *infinitely often.*

Again here examples abound: "the gate will be raised infinitely often" (F1), "if access to a critical section is infinitely often requested, then access will be granted infinitely often" (F2), etc. Remember that (F2) did not hold for the printer manager from section 1.3.

We also speak of *repeated liveness* (and sometimes of *repeated reachability*). This terminology is motivated by the various applications, from a methodological point of view, of properties which all have the same form (see section 10.2).

10.1 Fairness in Temporal Logic

Temporal logic is one of the most appropriate formalisms to express fairness properties. The $\overset{\infty}{F}$ combinator precisely corresponds to "an infinite number of times", or "infinitely often". An execution satisfies $\overset{\infty}{F} P$ if it infinitely often encounters a state in which P holds. Encountering a state satisfying P infinitely often is equivalent to finding states satisfying P arbitrarily far in the behavior: there is no last state in which P holds.

Example (F1) can be written $A \overset{\infty}{F}$ gate_raised, (F2) can be written $A(\overset{\infty}{F}$ crit_req $\Rightarrow \overset{\infty}{F}$ crit_in).

$\overset{\infty}{G}$, the dual of $\overset{\infty}{F}$, is also very useful. An execution satisfies $\overset{\infty}{G} P$ if P holds for all the states encountered, except possibly for a finite number of them, or equivalently, if P is always true from a certain point. An equivalent way of writing (F2) would be $A(\overset{\infty}{F}$ crit_in $\vee \ \overset{\infty}{G}$ ¬crit_req) which states that, along every behavior, either we traverse the critical section infinitely often ($\overset{\infty}{F}$ crit_in), or from a certain point on, we never request access again ($\overset{\infty}{G}$ ¬crit_req).

CTL *and fairness properties.* Note that fairness properties cannot be expressed in pure CTL. As explained in chapter 2, CTL prohibits the nesting of G and F (to obtain $\overset{\infty}{F}$) unless a path quantifier, A or E, is inserted between the G and the F. In the case of $A \overset{\infty}{F} P$, there is a way to respect the CTL syntax: $A \overset{\infty}{F} P$ is equivalent to $AG\, AF P$. But there is no such solution for $E \overset{\infty}{F} P$, nor for richer statements such as $E(\overset{\infty}{F} P_1 \wedge \overset{\infty}{F} P_2)$, etc.

This naturally leads to using "CTL+fairness", a CTL extension in which the $\overset{\infty}{F}$ and $\overset{\infty}{G}$ combinators are allowed (as well as their boolean combination). Technically speaking, in doing so we return to one of the various forms of the logic $ECTL^+$ first defined in [EH86], or to FCTL (read as *fair* CTL) introduced in [EL87].

From an algorithmic point of view, this extension is rather minor: model checking algorithms, be they enumerative or symbolic, are easily adapted. However the computation times increase and, as a rule, the amount of time required by the model checking is in $O(|\mathcal{A}| \times |\phi|^2)$ for CTL+fairness [EL87].

Many tools (like SMV) suggest considering the fairness hypotheses as part of the model rather than choosing CTL+fairness. This has no effect on model checking algorithms, but from a methodological viewpoint we may say that we (slightly) gain in simplicity, and that we (significantly) lose in flexibility and in expressive power (see section 10.5).

10.2 Fairness and Nondeterminism

In practice, fairness properties are very often used to describe the form of some nondeterministic sequences.

When a nondeterministic choice occurs at some point, this choice is often assumed to be *fair*: it is not biased in such a way as to consistently omit one option.

The simplest case to imagine is that of a die with six faces, which is repeatedly thrown. Its behavior is fair if it fulfills the property:

$$A \left(\overset{\infty}{F} 1 \wedge \overset{\infty}{F} 2 \wedge \overset{\infty}{F} 3 \wedge \overset{\infty}{F} 4 \wedge \overset{\infty}{F} 5 \wedge \overset{\infty}{F} 6 \right). \tag{10.1}$$

Note that this is a rather weak hypothesis which would be fulfilled by many biased dice (see below).

A statement that the die fulfills some sort of equiprobability would be much more ambitious and would require much more complex stochastic propositions and models. Fairness properties can be viewed as an abstraction of probabilistic properties. This abstraction is very useful, and proves sufficient in many practical cases: the arguments presented in section 8.2 in favor of using liveness properties apply in particular to fairness properties.

10.3 Fairness Properties and Fairness Hypotheses

As already seen in section 8.3 with regard to liveness properties, it is useful to distinguish between using temporal formulas as *hypotheses* and using them as *properties subject to verification*. Fairness properties are very often used as hypotheses.

An example. Consider a model of the classical alternating bit protocol. This involves a transmitter A, a receiver B, a line AB for the messages, and a line BA for message acknowledgements.

In this model, messages can be lost, and this is formalized by the non-deterministic behavior of the lines AB and BA: when they receive a message, they either transmit it or lose it.

It is possible to check the main safety properties on this model: any message received is indeed a message that was emitted earlier, and any sequence of received messages (beginning with the first) is indeed an initial portion of the sequence of emitted messages.

If we now try to establish liveness properties, such as "any emitted message is eventually received", we will probably fail. This is due to the fact that the model allows our unreliable lines to systematically lose all the messages. Obviously, such a behavior transmits no message at all.

But probably our intention was to model lines that are "unreliable" in a less radical sense: lines which, when they operate normally, may occasionally lose messages, for instance because of collisions, or spurious noise, etc. With this in mind, we do not wish to consider systematic message losses.

The simplest way to take such hypotheses into account is to restrict the nondeterministic choices "loss vs. transmission" in such a way that the lines do not systematically lose all their messages.

Consider a protocol in which one emitted message should normally correspond to several received messages. We will thus try to verify that the liveness property $G(\text{emitted} \Rightarrow F\,\text{received})$ is satisfied by all the fair behaviors, which is expressed as:

$$A\left(\overset{\infty}{F}\,\neg\text{loss} \;\Rightarrow\; G(\text{emitted} \Rightarrow F\,\text{received})\right)$$

An equivalent PLTL formulation is $\overset{\infty}{F}\,\neg\text{loss} \;\Rightarrow\; G(\text{emitted} \Rightarrow F\,\text{received})$, but the use of path quantifiers prevents misunderstandings. For example, it would not suffice to verify the property:

$$(A\,\overset{\infty}{F}\,\neg\text{loss}) \;\Rightarrow\; AG(\text{emitted} \Rightarrow F\,\text{received})$$

expressing that "if all the behaviors are fair, then all the behaviors verify the liveness property". Indeed this formula trivially holds for any model which produces at least one unfair behavior (since the premise of the implication is then false).

We have just described a situation in which a liveness property *subject to verification* depends on a fairness *hypothesis*. Of course there are some situations in which we wish to verify a fairness or a repeated liveness property. For example, we could check that the alternating bit protocol, under fair loss hypotheses, satisfies "if infinitely many messages are emitted, then infinitely many messages will be transmitted". We would then use the statement:

$$A\left(\overset{\infty}{F}\,\neg\texttt{loss} \;\Rightarrow\; (\overset{\infty}{F}\,\texttt{emitted} \Rightarrow \overset{\infty}{F}\,\texttt{received})\right)$$

The general form of this property is $A(\psi_1 \Rightarrow (\psi_2 \Rightarrow \phi))$, in which ψ_1 is the fairness hypothesis *per se*, and ψ_2 is a repeated liveness hypothesis which must imply ϕ, the repeated liveness property of interest.

Sometimes we wish to show that a system verifies a fairness property, without the help of fairness hypotheses on its behavior. There is nothing paradoxical about that. Imagine a simplistic implementation of a six-face die, which would sequentially produce the values 1, 2, ..., 6 in that order and would start over again.

Such a system is a kind of modulo 6 counter, totally deterministic, but which fully satisfies (10.1). The system surely verifies some much stronger properties, but if (10.1) is the only property we need, then it is (10.1) which we will prove! Of course this example is unrealistic; nevertheless it illustrates what happens with many scheduling algorithms: a scheduler often has a simple and deterministic behavior which suffices to guarantee a fairness property on its behaviors.

10.4 Strong Fairness and Weak Fairness

In the literature, we often find that a distinction is made between *strong fairness* and *weak fairness*. This terminology is rather classical. It applies to fairness properties of the form "if P is continually requested, then P will be granted (infinitely often)". A property of this form can be formalized in several ways.

Weak fairness. The first option views "P is continuously requested" as applying to situations in which P is requested *without interruption*. This interpretation precisely captures the weak fairness paradigm. We then obtain the statement $(\overset{\infty}{G}\,\texttt{requests\_}P) \Rightarrow FP$, or $(\overset{\infty}{G}\,\texttt{requests\_}P) \Rightarrow \overset{\infty}{F} P$. Note that both formulations become equivalent if they apply at any time:

$$G\left((\overset{\infty}{G}\,\texttt{requests\_}P) \Rightarrow FP\right) \;\equiv\; G\left((\overset{\infty}{G}\,\texttt{requests\_}P) \Rightarrow \overset{\infty}{F} P\right)$$

Strong fairness. A different interpretation views "P is continuously requested" as meaning more generally that P is requested in an infinitely repeated manner, possibly with interruptions. We then obtain the statement $(\overset{\infty}{F}\,\texttt{requests\_}P) \Rightarrow FP$, or $(\overset{\infty}{F}\,\texttt{requests\_}P) \Rightarrow \overset{\infty}{F} P$. Here also, both formulations become equivalent if they apply at any time:

$$G\left((\overset{\infty}{F}\,\texttt{requests\_}P) \Rightarrow FP\right) \;\equiv\; G\left((\overset{\infty}{F}\,\texttt{requests\_}P) \Rightarrow \overset{\infty}{F} P\right)$$

Strong/weak. The "strong/weak" terminology is explained by the fact that a strong fairness property implies the corresponding weak fairness property, while the converse is generally false. Moreover, constructing schedulers ensuring a weak fairness property is easier than doing it for strong fairness.

When using temporal logic for the model-checking of finite systems, there is no difference between strong and weak fairness. In this area, the strong/weak distinction is not relevant.

10.5 Fairness in the Model or in the Property?

Fairness properties have given rise to much research in the 1980's. An important motivation for this work was the search for models of concurrency with a fair parallel operation on components, in such a way that the problem illustrated by our example of figure 8.2 would never show up.

Developing such mathematical models is very intricate. Besides the technical problems encountered, one must choose the level at which the fairness hypotheses should apply: at the level of components? of groups of components? of transitions inside a component?

Moreover, once these choices are made, they are seldom satisfactory to whoever would like to verify properties with the help of a model checker. We very often wish to be able to modify the fairness hypotheses. In some cases we would like to strengthen them to be able to verify that a given property is satisfied. In other cases, we would like to ensure that the property to be checked is independent from all or part of the fairness hypotheses.

In most cases, the best way is to consider the model as a pair *automaton + fairness hypotheses* in which the second parameter can change independently from the first. This is the point of view which is adopted for example by SMV.

11. Abstraction Methods

By "abstraction methods" we mean a family of techniques which are used to simplify automata. The term *abstraction* refers to the nature of the simplifications performed, which generally consist in ignoring some aspects of the automaton involved.

The simplification may have different goals, but in this part of the book we only consider simplifications which aim at verifying a system (or verifying it faster) using a model checking approach. Thus we aim at reducing a complex problem "does $\mathcal{A} \models \phi$?" (Pb1) to a much simpler problem "does $\mathcal{A}' \models \phi'$?" (Pb2).

As explained in the first part of this book, the construction of a *formal model* of the underlying system is an abstraction process itself. But once our verification problem is formally expressed, for example in the form "does automaton $\mathcal{A}$ satisfy formula ϕ ?", it often turns out that the question cannot be solved by simple automatic model checking. Abstraction methods then come into play.

The benefit of this two-step procedure lies in the fact that it can in principle be formally justified: it is possible to state (and to prove mathematically) how the answers to (Pb2) are related to those of (Pb1). Here it is indeed the formulation (Pb1) which will be checked. Note that an approach which would directly come up with the simplified model $\mathcal{A}'$ would be further away from the original informal problem and would be more difficult to justify.

It is remarkable that a wealth of simplification methods used empirically in verification, often considered as non formal "tricks of the trade", can in fact be seen as abstraction methods amenable to a rigorous analysis.

Our message in this chapter is indeed precisely this: *the tricks of the trade used in simplification can be incorporated within a rigorous process.* We also wish to make it clear that precautions are required. With this in mind, we chose to illustrate the abstraction theme with simple examples rather than develop a theory. Any reader interested in a more formal presentation will find some answers in [CGL94b, DGG97].

11.1 When Is Model Abstraction Required?

Two main types of situations lead to the need for a simplified model:

Size of the automaton. The original model is too large to be verified by the tool at hand. This case is very frequent since model checking is subject to combinatorial explosion. This situation can result from the presence of too many variables, too many automata in parallel, or too many clocks in the timed automata.

Type of the automaton. The model checker at our disposal does not handle automata using a given construction: integer variables, communication channels, clocks, priorities, etc.

The following sections describe three classical abstraction methods.

11.2 Abstraction by State Merging

Abstraction by state merging consists in viewing some states of an automaton as identical. We also speak of *folding*, or *quotient*.

We can visualize state merging in a very concrete way: the merged states are put together in a kind of super-state. All the transitions leading out of one of the merged states (or into one) now lead out of the super-state (or into it).

Figure 11.1 depicts an example obtained from the digicode with error count used in chapter 1. The initial automaton $\mathcal{A}$ is shown on the left. We have circled the merged states with dotted lines. The result, $\mathcal{A}'$, is shown on the right.

$\mathcal{A}'$ is much more readable than $\mathcal{A}$. Not only has the number of states dropped from 17 to 5, but more importantly, the number of transitions has been reduced as a result of merging. It is clear from $\mathcal{A}'$ that the error counter must take all the values between 0 and 4 before the error state at the bottom of the diagram can be reached. Of course, in such a simple example, the same property is already easily extracted from the original automaton, especially since we have gone to the trouble of representing the states in a meaningful spatial arrangement. We will later come across several typical situations in which the advantage appears more clearly.

The most important question is *correctness*: some obvious properties of $\mathcal{A}'$ do not hold for $\mathcal{A}$! For example, all the states of $\mathcal{A}'$ can be reached through a path using only the letter A, and this does not hold for $\mathcal{A}$.

First of all, we tackle the correctness issue.

11.3 What Can Be Proved in the Abstract Automaton?

In general, and with some precautions to be spelled out later, we can use state merging *to verify safety properties*. This principle is explained by a few

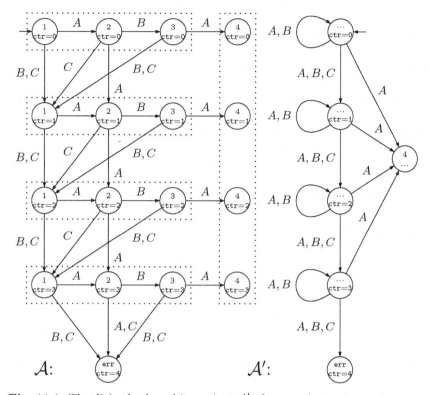

Fig. 11.1. The digicode $\mathcal{A}$, and its variant $\mathcal{A}'$ after merging

basic observations concerning the effect of merging states from an automaton $\mathcal{A}$ to obtain $\mathcal{A}'$:

1. $\mathcal{A}'$ has more behaviors than $\mathcal{A}$.
2. Now the more behaviors an automaton has, the fewer safety properties it fulfills.
3. Thus, if $\mathcal{A}'$ satisfies a safety property ϕ then *a fortiori* $\mathcal{A}$ satisfies ϕ.
4. However, if $\mathcal{A}'$ does not satisfy ϕ, no conclusions can be drawn about $\mathcal{A}$.

More behaviors. The automaton $\mathcal{A}'$ obtained by merging states shows more behaviors [1] than $\mathcal{A}$ does. On the one hand, all the executions of $\mathcal{A}$ remain present (perhaps in folded form) in $\mathcal{A}'$. On the other hand, some new behaviors may be introduced by the merging operation. In the digicode example, the transitions within the blocks give rise to loops in $\mathcal{A}'$. These loops make it possible, for instance, to remain indefinitely in the initial state.

---

[1] The notion of "more behaviors", already alluded to in section 7.2, may be defined formally for example in terms of *simulation*, a concept introduced and developed by R. Milner [Mil89]. Other definitions are possible. One must make sure that whichever definition is used does preserve safety properties.

Preserving safety properties. If $\mathcal{A}'$ satisfies a safety property ϕ, and if each execution of $\mathcal{A}$ is also an execution of $\mathcal{A}'$, then $\mathcal{A}$ also satisfies ϕ. This reminds us of the fact that the best way to satisfy a safety property is to do nothing (see chapter 7).

In the digicode example, it is necessary to ensure that the target property ϕ, namely "the error counter must take all the values between 0 and 4 before the error state can be reached", is indeed a safety property, otherwise our analysis of $\mathcal{A}'$ would be irrelevant.

Guaranteeing that ϕ is indeed a safety property is far from obvious. It can be done by writing ϕ in the form $\mathsf{AG}\phi^-$, based on an alternative formulation of the property, for example "in the error state, we have necessarily had $\mathtt{ctr} = 4$ earlier and $\mathtt{ctr} = 3$ yet earlier and so on until $\mathtt{ctr} = 0$". This leads to

$$\mathsf{AG}(\ \mathtt{err} \Rightarrow$$
$$\mathsf{F}^{-1}(\mathtt{ctr=4} \wedge \mathsf{F}^{-1}(\mathtt{ctr=3} \wedge \mathsf{F}^{-1}(\mathtt{ctr=2} \wedge \mathsf{F}^{-1}(\mathtt{ctr=1} \wedge \mathsf{F}^{-1}\mathtt{ctr=0})))))$$
$$(11.1)$$

One-way preservation. $\mathcal{A}'$ can be used to verify a safety property, but not to invalidate it. If $\mathcal{A}'$ does not satisfy ϕ, then it satisfies $\neg\phi$. But the negation of a safety property is in general not a safety property.

By looking at the behaviors of $\mathcal{A}'$, we can better understand why preservation is one-way. Imagine that ϕ does not hold in $\mathcal{A}'$. Then some behaviors of $\mathcal{A}'$ are unsafe. However, these behaviors may originate from the folding, and perhaps they don't occur in $\mathcal{A}$. Thus we cannot conclude that $\mathcal{A}$ necessarily has unsafe behaviors. (Accordingly, if we wish to show that a safety property *is not satisfied* by $\mathcal{A}$, then merging states cannot help us.)

We are facing an instance of a more general situation: abstraction methods are often *one-way*. A user intent on verifying a safety property can rely on state merging only if he obtains a positive answer to his question. If the answer is negative, then he learned nothing about $\mathcal{A}$.

Nonetheless, information can sometimes be drawn from the diagnostic provided by the model checker. When $\mathcal{A}'$ does not satisfy ϕ, analyzing the diagnostic sometimes yields a behavior showing that $\mathcal{A}$ fails to satisfy ϕ for the same reasons. And even if no such reconstruction is possible, the diagnostic can suggest a finer way of merging the states of $\mathcal{A}$.

Some necessary precautions. There is a difficulty which we have skimmed over so far. The informal description of the merging operation did not explain how the atomic propositions labelling the states were to be gathered on the super-states resulting from the merging. We left out this aspect from the example on figure 11.1 on purpose.

This problem has a theoretical answer. In principle, *we must never merge states that are not labelled with the same properties*. The theorem guaranteeing that $\mathcal{A}$ satisfies all the safety properties satisfied by $\mathcal{A}'$ hinges on this hypothesis.

This is a rather strong restriction, clearly violated by the merging performed on our digicode example (See figure 11.1).

Now a refined understanding allows us to weaken this restriction. The following remark first comes to mind: if merging is used to check a given property ϕ, then only the propositions occurring in ϕ are relevant.

This remark may seem trivial but the situations in which it applies are numerous. In the digicode example, merging respects the err labels (we never merged a state labelled err with a state not satisfying it). It is thus possible to verify on $\mathcal{A}'$ a safety property in which only the proposition err comes into play, for example "an error state cannot be the successor of an error state", which can be expressed as $\mathsf{AG}(\mathtt{err} \Rightarrow \mathsf{X}^{-1}\neg\mathtt{err})$.

Some situations are more complicated. For example, the property of interest, in our digicode, involved err and the propositions $\mathtt{ctr} = \ldots$ based on counter values. The latter propositions are not preserved by the merging on figure 11.1. Indeed, the four states in the block on the right are merged although they carry different $\mathtt{ctr} = \ldots$ properties. We must therefore bring in an additional argument in order to prove the validity of our procedure.

If a proposition P *only appears in positive form* in ϕ (that is, each occurrence of P is within an even number of negation symbols, see examples below), then we can merge states without the need for these to agree on the presence of P. The resulting super-state will carry the label P if and only if all the merged states carried it. On figure 11.1, we have marked a super-state with $\ldots$ to indicate the absence of a label as a consequence of the label only appearing on a subset of the merged states.

In the digicode example, we were interested in the property formalized as (11.1). In such a formula, all the occurrences of the $\mathtt{ctr} = \ldots$ propositions are positive. Therefore it is correct to use $\mathcal{A}' \models \phi$ to conclude that $\mathcal{A} \models \phi$ although the merging of the four states on the right of $\mathcal{A}$ leads to the removal of some $\mathtt{ctr} = \ldots$ labels.

We can explain this method by splitting it into two steps: (1) we remove some labels from some states, resulting in a reduction of the number of safety properties satisfied (here, we only refer to the safety properties in which the labels removed appear positively), then (2) we merge the states that now have the same labels.

The other way round, we may add propositions if these only occur negatively in ϕ. Some general words of caution are: unless these techniques are automated, they can often be an important source of error. Indeed, it is not always obvious to tell whether a proposition appears negatively. For instance, in $\mathsf{AG}(P \Leftrightarrow Q)$, both propositions each have a positive and a negative occurrence: $P \Leftrightarrow Q$ is short for $(P \Rightarrow Q) \wedge (Q \Rightarrow P)$ and $P \Rightarrow Q$ means $(\neg P) \vee Q$.

Modularity. State merging is preserved by product. If $\mathcal{A}'$ is obtained from $\mathcal{A}$ by merging states, then the product automaton $\mathcal{A}' \parallel \mathcal{B}$ is also obtained from $\mathcal{A} \parallel \mathcal{B}$ by a merging operation.

Without this modularity property, the benefits of merging would be reduced. After all, we apply merging to a system because its size prevents us from manipulating it while using a model checker. But if we must indeed construct the automaton before we can simplify it, the same size problems will arise.

The modularity of merging makes it possible to reduce the components of a network of automata before computing their product automaton. The digicode example is simplistic, but if this automaton is a mere component of a larger system, then the simplification performed above may reduce the total number of states by a factor of 2 or 3.

State merging in practice. State merging as described leads to the following question: how will we guess and then specify the sets of states to be merged when the automaton contains a large number of states?

None of the tools presented in the third part of this book offers any assistance for merging states. Note that the situation is different with the tools developed around process algebras, such as the *Concurrency Workbench* [CPS93]. These tools have the ability to automatically (and modularly) reduce the automata according to a bisimilarity criterion, which is sometimes too strong because it preserves all behavioral properties.

In practice, the user is the one who defines and applies his own abstractions. Such work can be tedious and error-prone. (We can thus loudly lament over the lack of assistance offered to perform this merging, all the more so since it would be rather easy for a tool to apply the merging requested by a user.)

When the system is described by an automaton dealing with variables, the merging operation is often described by an abstraction on the variables, which is easy to define and, especially, to implement. This is the topic of the next section.

11.4 Abstraction on the Variables

Abstraction on the variables is an abstraction technique which concerns the "data" part (as opposed to the "control" part) of automata with variables.

An asset of variable abstraction is that it directly applies to the description of the automata with variables. Folding the automaton is therefore not necessary, which often proves crucial to the extent that abstraction aims at the verification of large systems.

The variable abstractions we describe in this chapter all apply to unfolded automata. However, the technique is more general and leads to other notions of abstraction as well.

An example. The example of the digicode with error counting, from figure 11.1, is in fact obtained by unfolding the automaton with variables depicted on figure 11.2.

var ctr : int;

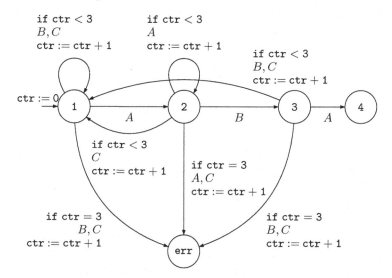

Fig. 11.2. The digicode before unfolding

Suppose that automata with variables cannot be specified with our tool. We can overcome this problem by *coding* the variables one way or the other. This often amounts to performing the unfolding by hand.

An approximate solution consists in simply *ignoring the variables*. We then remove the guards since these refer to the variables, and we remove as well the instructions updating the variables, such as ctr := ctr + 1. In the case of the digicode, we would obtain the automaton depicted on figure 11.3, which can be viewed as a *skeleton* of the initial automaton.

Deleting variables. A remarkable consequence of such an operation is that the automaton $\mathcal{A}'$ obtained by removing all mentions of the variables from an automaton $\mathcal{A}$ inherits more behaviors than $\mathcal{A}$. Thus all the safety properties satisfied by $\mathcal{A}'$ are *a fortiori* satisfied by $\mathcal{A}$, or more precisely, by the automaton obtained from unfolding $\mathcal{A}$.

This situation is easy to see: with respect to the behavior of the skeleton, the effect of the variables is mostly to forbid the execution of some transitions in the configurations in which the guard is not fulfilled. Removing the guards yields more behaviors.

In this way, deleting variables is an abstraction method whose theoretical basis is similar to that of abstraction by merging. One of the strengths of

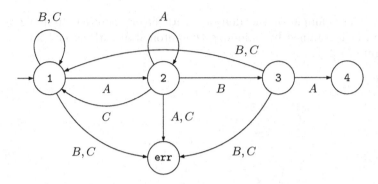

Fig. 11.3. The digicode without the variables (nor the guards)

deletion is the great simplicity of its implementation. Its main weakness is its coarseness: in most cases, the variables and the guards are obviously necessary to guarantee that the target property holds, while programs which manipulate variables without depending on them are rare in practice (they are more common in the theory in which they are called *data-independent programs*). We will see later how to make more subtle deletions.

Practical aspects. If variables are removed because a tool cannot handle them, all of them will be removed. If the motivation is to avoid a combinatorial explosion problem in the unfolding, then we may choose to delete some variables and keep some others. In this case, modifying the guards may be difficult when deleted and remaining variables both appear: when in doubt, it is always possible to delete more guards.

A more delicate problem concerns the properties which label the states. When we inspect the unfolded automaton arising from an automaton with variables, we often find atomic propositions which refer to the values of the variables. For example, in the digicode, we used propositions such as $ctr = 4$. Deleting some variables of course forbids using them in the safety property that we aim at verifying. In practice, this bothersome limitation is often circumvented by more or less *ad hoc* coding.

Abstraction differs from deletion. When we wish to simplify the treatment of variables by an abstraction approach, we can appeal to less brutal techniques than outright deletion.

These techniques pertain to *abstract interpretation*, the mathematical theory aiming at defining, analyzing, and justifying methods, based on abstraction, for the approximate computation of program properties.

We do not wish to describe the theory in detail (see for example [Cou96]). However, the concrete verification of large systems naturally leads to reinventing and using a number of rather simple variable manipulations. We would like to describe the manipulations here, keeping in mind that a formal framework exists to explain them.

Bounded variables. A strategy which is widely to simplify an automaton whose unfolding would result in state explosion is to narrow down the domain of the variables. The gain is obvious when going from an integer variable (in principle, infinitely many values) to a variable restricted to a finite integer interval, for instance all values from 0 to 10.

This kind of simplification also applies to potentially unbounded communication channels for which we choose to limit the maximal size (as in the SPIN tool, see chapter 13).

Intuition suggests that, when bounding the domain of a variable v of an automaton $\mathcal{A}$, one obtains an automaton $\mathcal{A}'$ whose behavior is not totally different from that of $\mathcal{A}$. In fact, thanks to an appropriate modification of the guards, it is sometimes possible to guarantee that $\mathcal{A}'$ again has more behaviors than $\mathcal{A}$, so that the satisfaction of safety properties can be transferred from $\mathcal{A}'$ to $\mathcal{A}$.

For this it suffices that the unfolding of the automaton $\mathcal{A}'$ be obtainable by merging states from the unfolding of $\mathcal{A}$, which will be the case whenever the values of the variable v in $\mathcal{A}'$ can be viewed as corresponding to equivalence classes of its values in $\mathcal{A}$.

A very simple example is provided by the digicode. We can restrict the possible values of ctr to the interval 0..1, with the interpretation that these are values modulo 2 (see figure 11.4).

var ctr:0..1;

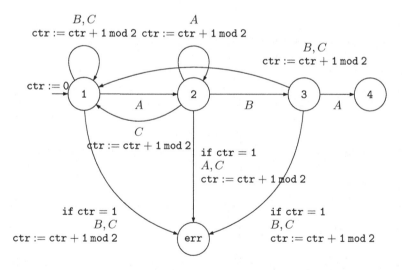

Fig. 11.4. The digicode with a modulo 2 counter

Looking at figure 11.4, we can notice that the guards and the update operations on the variables have been modified according to the new interpretation modulo 2 given to ctr. This operation is often delicate ; it is simplified in our example by the fact that addition behaves well in combination with equivalence modulo 2. Note that the guards if ctr = 3 and if ctr < 3 have been replaced, respectively, by if ctr = 1 and true (omitted). A guard if ctr ≠ 3 would not be replaced by if ctr ≠ 1 but also by true.

We do not wish to dwell further on the theoretical details, but we have to mention that these manipulations can become rather subtle. A principle which must constantly guide the user is the *necessity to ensure that the simplified system has more behaviors than the original system*.

When bounded means limited. The simplification obtained by bounding the variables initially defined on a huge domain, for example all integers, is very often used in practice. Users generally don't see the simplification as an abstraction such as counting modulo k but rather as a behavior restriction induced by certain limits which cannot be exceeded. Finally, there is the same conceptual link between an automaton $\mathcal{A}$ and its bounded variant $\mathcal{A}'$ as between an abstract algorithm and its implementation on a computer having a bounded memory.

From a theoretical point of view, if $\mathcal{A}'$ is obtained from $\mathcal{A}$ by bounding some of its variables, then a *restriction* was applied to the system, and this precludes transferring safety properties in one direction or the other (see section 11.5). In practice, the verification of a bounded variant dramatically increases our confidence in the system, much in the way that testing does. Moreover, an error uncovered via the bounded variant can often be extended to the original automaton.

It turns out that it is rather easy to reconcile this very pragmatic approach with the general framework of variable abstractions.

Let us return to the digicode example and restrict the variable ctr to the interval 0..2. This restriction can be viewed as an abstraction if we interpret the value 2 as *"any integer greater than or equal to 2"*. This interpretation forces us, as in the "modulo 2" case, to modify guards and variable assignments. For example, an assignment ctr := ctr + 1 will become ctr := min(ctr + 1, 2). The resulting automaton is depicted on figure 11.5.

Once the guards and the assignments are corrected with interpretation *"2 represents any integer greater or equal to 2"*, we can assert that any safety property satisfied by $\mathcal{A}'$ is satisfied by $\mathcal{A}$.

11.5 Abstraction by Restriction

Restriction is a particular form of simplification that operates by forbidding some behaviors of the system or by making some impossible.

In practice, we can restrict an automaton by removing states, transitions, by strengthening the guards, etc. We can also restrict the system by bounding

var ctr : 0..2 ;

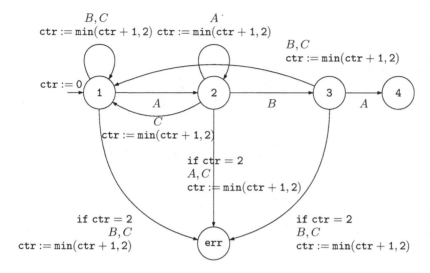

Fig. 11.5. The digicode with a counter bounded by 2

the variables, but then we do not reinterpret the bounds as we have done in the example on figure 11.5.

Finally, a technique often used consists in removing all the transitions carrying a given label. For instance, it is possible to remove all the transitions labelled A from the digicode automaton. The resulting automaton is depicted on figure 11.6.

Clearly, state 4 is no longer reachable. States 2 and 3 have also become unreachable. Indeed the unfolded automaton has become very simple, see figure 11.7.

What the restrictions preserve. If $\mathcal{A}'$ is obtained from $\mathcal{A}$ by restriction, then literally all the behaviors of $\mathcal{A}'$ are behaviors of $\mathcal{A}$. Thus if $\mathcal{A}'$ does not satisfy a safety property, then *a fortiori* neither does $\mathcal{A}$.

An equivalent but more positive way to present this result is to say that conditional reachability properties, such as EF err, which are negations of safety properties, can be checked on the restricted automaton. In the digicode example, the automaton $\mathcal{A}'$ from figure 11.6 clearly satisfies EF err. We conclude that $\mathcal{A}$ also satisfies this property.

The main feature of restrictions is indeed this "inverse" preservation. We can use the restrictions to prove that a safety property does not hold (that is, to find errors) but not to prove the correctness of $\mathcal{A}$.

The great advantage of restrictions is their simplicity, both conceptual and implementational. Moreover, restriction is a modular operation: if $\mathcal{A}'$

var ctr : int;

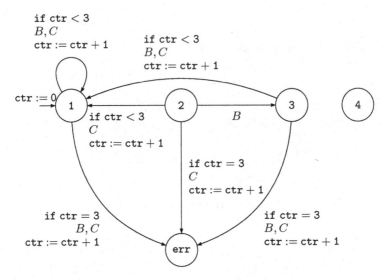

Fig. 11.6. The digicode with no A transition

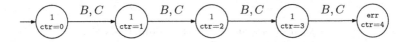

Fig. 11.7. The unfolding of the digicode with no A transition

is a restriction of $\mathcal{A}$, then the synchronous composition $\mathcal{A}' \parallel \mathcal{B}$ will be a restriction of $\mathcal{A} \parallel \mathcal{B}$.

An important aspect of the method just illustrated is that it naturally applies to an automaton with variables. The implementation is then easy, but some of the more subtle restrictions can only be defined at the level of the unfolded automaton. In the next section we describe a method that offers more flexibility in restricting the behavior of the automaton.

Note however that certain tools, like DESIGN/CPN, allow a parametric construction of the set of reachable states, by using a local halting condition (see chapter 14). With such a feature, it is possible to build restrictions that depend on flexible criteria, expressed in terms of the states of the unfolded automaton rather than those of the initial automaton.

11.6 Observer Automata

The method of *observer automata* aims at simplifying a system by restricting its legitimate behaviors to those accepted by an automaton outside the system, called *observer automaton* (or also *testing automaton*).

Compared to the restriction methods seen earlier, the observers method reduces the size of an automaton by restricting its *behaviors* rather than its structure (the states and the transitions).

An example. Consider our digicode again. As it is too simple to illustrate the power of observer automata, we shall use a somewhat artificial problem.

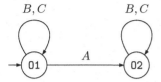

Fig. 11.8. $\mathcal{O}$, an observer automaton for the digicode

Suppose that our "no A transition" restriction is not sufficient to establish the desired reachability property. Suppose further that we have some reasons to believe that the desired property can be proved by only considering the behaviors in which a single A may occur (the number of occurrences of B and C remains arbitrary). An automaton $\mathcal{O}$ accepting this type of behavior is given in figure 11.8.

It is now possible to synchronize the digicode and the observer $\mathcal{O}$. The result is depicted on figure 11.9, in which we have only kept the reachable states so as to present a clear figure.

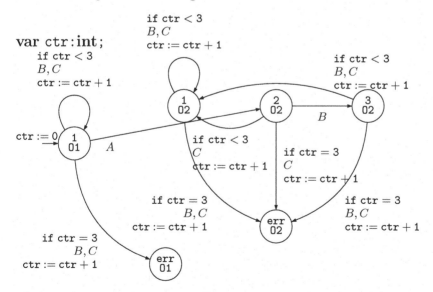

Fig. 11.9. The synchronized digicode with its observer

The result is a little more complicated than the initial automaton but its behaviors are restricted. Unfolding the automaton of figure 11.9 yields the system which is represented on figure 11.10.

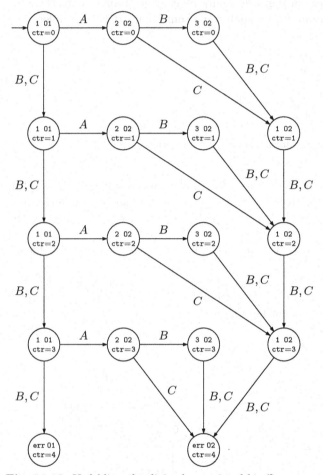

Fig. 11.10. Unfolding the digicode restricted by $\mathcal{O}$

Compared to the unfolding of the digicode found in figure 11.1, the *number of paths* has been reduced here. The number of states can increase because of the fact that the observer automaton adds a component. The worst possible case leads in principle to a blowup of the number of states by a multiplicative factor of $|\mathcal{O}|$. In practice, on automata which are more complicated than the digicode, we obtain a definite reduction when unfolding.

Our example was very simple, but the method is general and powerful. It enables us to use very rich observer automata (with history variables, counters, etc.). The synchronization can be done in other ways than via the transition labels, and constructions based on the propositions or the values of variables are possible. Since the observer does not add behaviors, the satisfaction of reachability properties can be transferred from the abstract automaton to the initial one.

Observer automata and temporal logic. In this section we have used observer automata to restrict the behavior of an automaton and, for the sake of simplicity, we have not mentioned their more advanced uses.

Actually, the scope of the technique is more general. When an automaton $\mathcal{A}$ is synchronized with an observer $\mathcal{O}$, it is possible to read some information on the form of the path followed, from the control states of $\mathcal{O}$. Accordingly, the reachability of a given control state of $\mathcal{O}$ provides information on the occurrence of a particular behavior of $\mathcal{A}$.

Finally, observe that the model checking algorithm of PLTL (see chapter 3) can be viewed as a sophisticated use of the concept of observer automata.

Conclusion

In practice, verification by model checking requires a good deal of expertise from the user. Far from being a quasi-magical "push-button" approach, it quickly comes up against difficult obstacles to overcome.

Some of the limitations of model checking will gradually subside as a result of technological advances (better tools, better algorithms, etc.). In the meantime, the user must invest a lot of effort to formulate his problem in a form which is able to circumvent the shortcomings of the available tool. This aspect of the work is more akin to art than to science, hence the difficulty.

The concepts presented and, especially, illustrated in the second part of the book, should constitute a valuable asset.

The *classification of properties* helps charting a course through the jungle of temporal formulas. In practice, a few broad families of properties, corresponding to a small number of linguistic constructs, uniformly cover the vast majority of properties likely to find their way into a set of requirements. A second source of interest in such a classification is practical. Verifying a safety property and verifying a fairness property call on different strategies.

Next, the various *simplification methods*, applied to automata and in ubiquitous use today, can be justified formally. Such a task adds credence to the methods, while delimiting their application domains and bringing some indispensable precautions to the fore.

In conclusion, we would like to stress (and lament) the fact that current tools do not provide any assistance worthy of the name when it comes to simplifying automata. Such assistance would help avoiding conceptual mistakes and would render simplification less tedious to implement. We can only wish that the increasing popularity of model checking techniques will lead to the development of true all-inclusive computer-assisted formal verification environments.

Part III

Some Tools

Part III

Source Code

Introduction

The concepts and algorithms presented in the first part of this book take effect in software tools, namely *model checkers*. During the past few years, errors have been discovered, when using these model checkers, within larger and larger systems. The success and limitations of these tools lead to an important research activity in the field of verification. Although this research has a high theoretical level, it systematically faces reality through the development of new tools, with increasing efficiency.

In the third part, we have chosen to present six tools, used nowadays for verification around the world. Each of these tools is concerned with a particular application domain, and we do not intend to compare them, even less so to classify them. Nevertheless, we will not hide their drawbacks as we perceive them.

Our choice has focused on SMV, SPIN, DESIGN/CPN, UPPAAL, KRONOS and HYTECH. This choice is consistent with the following aims:

Academic tools: these are tools in the core of the development of new methods and theories for model checking. They propose implementations of new, original and very promising techniques, which will certainly be available, in one form or another, in the next generation of industrial tools.

Freely available tools: all the selected tools are available free of charge via the Internet. The reader can test the tool he wants on any problem he is interested in, and a lecturer can freely use any of these tools within his courses.

Tools used by a lot of teams: each tool has a community of users which is greater, sometime much greater, than the group from which the tool originates. This is a strong argument, which underlines the unrefutable usefulness of the tool. It is also a way to objectively evaluate the pros and cons of tools. Note that being freely available helps the dissemination of tools.

Our choice to consider only tools issued from universities does have some consequences. They all present some very typical limitations: the tool is not available for all platforms, there is no organized user support, the graphical user interface is sometimes very rude, etc. In general, the authors of these tools preferred to develop an original algorithm to solve a difficult problem rather than enhance the ergonomics or portability. If one accepts these limitations, one can take advantage of brand new techniques which are not yet available in the industrial tools of older design. In a few years' time, the most efficient tools used in industry will certainly be inspired by today's academic tools.

How to read these chapters. Each tool is presented independently of the others. We assume that the reader is familiar with the theoretical basis described in the first part. We explicitly refer to the latter only in a few very precise cases.

We systematically illustrate each tool description by an example, so as to quickly give an idea of the tool capabilities. Of course, our presentation does not describe all the aspects of the tools: particular features, specific algorithms, etc. Each presentation ends with a bibliography which can be used by the interested reader to obtain more information.

12. SMV – Symbolic Model Checking

SMV has been developed by K. L. McMillan under the guidance of E. M. Clarke at Carnegie-Mellon University (Pittsburgh, PA, USA). It performs (BDD-based) symbolic model checking of CTL formulae on networks of automata with shared variables. The tool is available via the Internet [1].

12.1 What Can We Do with SMV?

SMV's input is a network of automata that act mostly on shared variables. Hierarchical constructions are possible, allowing one to compose automata. Automata are described textually. Fairness assumptions can be included. Then one can verify whether the system satisfies temporal properties written in CTL. In the cases in which a requested property is not satisfied, SMV provides an example run that violates the property.

SMV offers many options allowing its user to try several different strategies for the ordering of boolean variables, for the representation of the state graph, etc.

12.2 SMV's Essentials

SMV is the first model checker which used the BDD technology and thus managed to check *exhaustively* that *very large* systems did indeed fulfill their CTL specifications.

On top of the ergonomy problems shared by all academic tools, one limitation of SMV is its lack of simulation facilities. We could also criticize the language chosen for describing the automata and the networks of automata: SMV is better suited to the description of a Kripke structure to be encoded in BDDs than of systems built hierarchically by juxtaposing and synchronizing finite automata. As a consequence, the validity of the specified model is more problematic than usual.

---

[1] See http://www.cs.cmu.edu/~modelcheck/smv.html.

Conclusion. SMV is one of the tools which is most likely to be able to fully check a complex system, but its limits on the pragmatic side can appear as a problem in some situations.

12.3 Describing Automata

SMV's language for the description of automata adopts a very declarative viewpoint that can be confusing. Its conception is clearly oriented towards describing a "possible next state" relation between states seen as tuples of values.

We now describe a simplified elevator model. The following lines:

```
MODULE main
VAR
    cabin : 0 .. 3;
    dir : {up,down};
```

declare two variables: `cabin` that records the position of the elevator cabin, and `dir` that indicates its direction. The position is a floor number between 0 and 3. In SMV, all variables have a finite domain, thus guaranteeing the finiteness of the state space.

The global state of the system also indicates, for each $0 \leq i \leq 3$, whether there is a pending request for floor i. This is stored in an array of booleans, another finite domain variable:

```
VAR
    request : array 0 .. 3 of boolean;
```

If we use no other variable, our system has $4 \times 2 \times 2^4 = 128$ possible states.

Operational description of transitions. After the states, we now have to define the transition relation. The simplest way SMV offers for this is to define a `next` relation. Here, the `next` notation applies to variables and not to the complete state, which allows us to decompose the changes into several parts. Let us start with the description of the cabin moves in our model: in the simplified model, the cabin goes up and then down according to the infinite sequence 0, 1, 2, 3, 2, 1, 0, 1, 2, 3, 2, etc.

```
ASSIGN
    next(cabin):=case
                    dir = up & cabin < 3   : cabin + 1; -- moves up
                    dir = down & cabin > 0 : cabin - 1; -- moves down
                    1 : cabin;                          -- stuck
                esac;
    next(dir)  :=case
                    dir = up & cabin = 2   : down;      -- switch dir
                    dir = down & cabin = 1 : up;        -- switch dir
                    1 : dir;                            -- keep on
                esac;
```

Assigning a value to "next(cabin)" as a function of cabin and dir really describes how the value of the cabin variable *in a next state* depends on the *current values* of cabin and dir. The "case ... esac" construction is a disjunction over cases where the first valid left-hand side is selected, and in which the final "1" is an always-valid left-hand side, indicating the default clause. There is a similar description of how dir evolves.

An equivalent way of describing the evolution of dir would be:

```
next(dir):=case
            dir = up & next(cabin) = 3   : down;   -- switch dir
            dir = down & next(cabin) = 0 : up;     -- switch dir
            1 : dir;                                -- keep on
        esac;
```

This definition, that we find clearer, relies on the value of next(cabin) to define the value of next(dir). Observe that SMV allows such a definition to occur before the definition of next(cabin). In fact, these next(...) definitions should not be understood with an imperative assignment semantics. SMV has a very declarative semantics and it understands any boolean formula linking current and future values of the variables.

We describe how requests evolve in a similar way. The simplified model allows a request for some floor to appear at any time *except if the cabin is actually on this floor*. Then a request cannot disappear until the cabin does reach that floor, in which case the request immediately disappears (that is, is satisfied).

```
next(request[0]) := case
                    next(cabin) = 0 : 0;   -- disappears
                    request[0] : 1;        -- remains
                    1 : {0,1};             -- may appear
                esac;
next(request[1]) := case
                    next(cabin) = 1 : 0;   -- disappears
                    ........
```

The definition uses the "{0,1}" construct to indicate a set of possible values for next(request[0]). The system is non-deterministic. In this example, non-determinism is used to model a freely evolving environment.

Description of initial states. The initial values of variables are declared according to a similar mechanism:

```
init(cabin)      := 0;
init(dir)        := up;
init(request[0]) := 0;
...
```

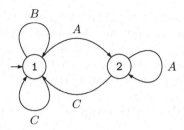

Fig. 12.1. Example of an automaton

Description of control states. SMV lacks the concept of "control state" that we often use. Figure 12.1 shows a part of the digicode example.

Describing this automaton in SMV would require the explicit use of a "current state" variable, ranging over a finite set (e.g., an enumerated type). Then we would have to introduce an error state to describe automata in which some states have no successors. For example, we would write:

```
VAR
  state : {q1, q2, qerror};
  key : {A, B, C};
ASSIGN
  next(state) := case
                   state = q1 & (key = B | key = C) : q1;
                   state = q1 & key = A : q2;
                   state = q2 & key = A : q2;
                   state = q2 & key = C : q1;
                   1 : qerror;
                 esac;
```

We would still have to define how **key** evolves with time. Obviously this machinery is quite heavy when it comes to describing transitions between control states of automata.

Declarative description of transitions. SMV offers another more declarative way of defining initial states and transition relations.

Initial states can be defined by giving a characteristic property (an arbitrary boolean formula), for example:

```
INIT
  (dir = up & cabin = 0)
```

This formula does not constrain the initial values of the **request[i]**, thus all values are possible.

A similar construction can be used for the transition relation. For example, one can characterize the set of situations where the direction of the cabin does not change, by writing:

```
TRANS
  (next(dir) = dir) <-> (!(next(cabin) = 0) & !(next(cabin) = 3))
```

```
-- specification AG AF (!request[0] & !request[1] & !requ...
-- is false as demonstrated by the following execution sequence
state 1.1:
cabin = 0
dir = up
request[0] = 0
request[1] = 0
request[2] = 0
request[3] = 0

-- loop starts here --
state 1.2:
cabin = 1
request[3] = 1

state 1.3:
cabin = 2

state 1.4:
cabin = 3
dir = down
request[2] = 1
request[3] = 0

state 1.5:
cabin = 2
request[2] = 0
request[3] = 1

state 1.6:
cabin = 1

state 1.7:
cabin = 0
dir = up

state 1.8:
cabin = 1
```

Fig. 12.2. Error diagnostic provided by SMV

Observe that all these declarations, together with the definitions introduced by ASSIGN, are combined. They then "add up" meaning that each new
declaration further restricts the set of initial states and/or possible transitions.

12.4 Verification

We now have completely defined the automaton that we wish to analyze, and
it is possible to submit it to the CTL model checker. The syntax for CTL is

essentially the one we presented in chapter 2. Here we only use the temporal operators AG, for "it always holds that ...", and AF, for "inevitably ...".

Let us verify that our elevator model has no deadlock:

```
SPEC
  AG EX 1        -- NB: 1 denotes << true >> in SMV
```

We get the answer :

```
-- specification AG EX 1 is true
```

Similarly one can check that "all requests are eventually satisfied":

```
SPEC
  AG(AF!request[0] & AF!request[1] & AF!request[2] & AF!request[3])
```

If we ask to check that "requests are eventually all satisfied (simultaneously)" with:

```
SPEC
  AG AF (!request[0] & !request[1] & !request[2] & !request[3])
```

SMV provides an error diagnostic (given in figure 12.2) under the form of an (ultimately) cyclic run in which requests for floors 2 and 3 appear as soon as the elevator leaves one of the floors. In this run, states are listed in succession until the loop is closed. Each state is concisely described by only giving the values of the components that have been modified while moving from the previous state.

12.5 Synchronizing Automata

For the construction of networks of automata, the viewpoint adopted by SMV is inspired by logical circuits (without the graphical aspects). As an example, let us consider the network schematized in figure 12.3.

SMV describes each component of this network as an automaton in which output channels are actually state variables in which the automaton can write, and where input channels are parameters that stand for other variables in other components.

Automaton A2 from figure 12.3 is described as follows:

```
MODULE A2(in1,in2)              -- in1, in2 are inputs
VAR
  out: boolean;                 -- for example
  othervar : 0 .. 9;            -- a variable local to A2
ASSIGN
  next (out) := case            -- update output
              in1 = in2 : 0;    -- read inputs
              ...
```

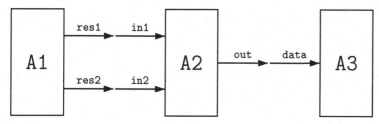

Fig. 12.3. A communicating automata network

The global architecture of the network is defined via:

```
MODULE main
VAR
  elem1 : A1;
  elem2 : A2(elem1.res1,elem1.res2);
  elem3 : A3(elem2.out);
  other_local_vars : ...
SPEC
  (elem2.out = 1) -> ...
  ...
```

Thus modules are seen as variables of "record" type, that import their own variables. One can use several instances of the same module.

Synchronous and asynchronous networks. The example we just considered assumes a network of three synchronous modules: a transition in the global system involves a transition in every component. This point of view is suitable for logical circuits.

In SMV modules can evolve in an asynchronous way: a transition of the global system is a transition of one and only one component. This behavior is obtained by using the keyword PROCESS in place of the MODULE in our example.

In order to allow stating assumptions on the way they are scheduled, each component provides an additional boolean variable called "**running**". In a given state, P.**running** is true if and only if P is the component involved in the transition. Then, temporal logic formulae can state properties and assumptions about scheduling by referring to these **running** variables.

12.6 Documentation and Case Studies

The SMV manual is available on the Internet. It has not been updated and is not very user friendly. The book *Symbolic Model Checking* [McM93] is a much better introduction, with examples of impressive size.

Several case studies conducted with SMV are available in the literature. Some case studies from the SMV group itself give a good idea of the tool capabilities:

- the Gigamax cache coherence protocol [MS92];
- the Futurebus+ cache coherence protocol [CGH$^+$95];
- a logical circuit with 10^{1300} states [CGL94].

The case studies conducted by other groups adopt the point of view of the user, who is concerned with the verification of a given system, and they underline the strengths and weaknesses of SMV:

- a commutation system [FHS95];
- a component of the T9000 processor [Bar95];
- cache coherence protocols [WV95];
- several versions of the alternating bit protocol [BK95];
- various systems: protocols, logic circuits, software, PLCs [GKKN94, Moo94].

SMV Bibliography

[Bar95]   G. Barrett. Model checking in practice: The T9000 virtual channel processor. *IEEE Transactions on Software Engineering*, 21(2):69–78, 1995.

[BK95]   A. Biere and A. Kick. A case study on different modelling approaches based on model checking - verifying numerous versions of the alternating bit protocol with SMV. Technical Report 95-5, Universität Karlsruhe, Germany, February 1995.

[CGH$^+$95] E. M. Clarke, O. Grumberg, H. Hiraishi, S. Jha, D. E. Long, K. L. McMillan, and L. A. Ness. Verification of the Futurebus+ cache coherence protocol. *Formal Methods in System Design*, 6(2):217–232, 1995.

[CGL94]   E. M. Clarke, O. Grumberg, and D. E. Long. Model checking and abstraction. *ACM Transactions on Programming Languages and Systems*, 16(5):1512–1542, 1994.

[FHS95]   A. R. Flora-Holmquist and M. G. Staskauskas. Formal validation of virtual finite state machines. In *Proc. Workshop on Industrial-Strength Formal Specification Techniques (WIFT'95), Boca Raton, FL*, pages 122–129, April 1995.

[GKKN94] G. Gopalakrishnan, D. Khandekar, R. Kuramkote, and R. Nalumasu. Case studies in symbolic model checking. Technical Report UUCS-94-009, University of Utah, Department of Computer Science, Salt Lake City, UT, USA, March 1994.

[McM93]   K. L. McMillan. *Symbolic Model Checking*. Kluwer Academic, 1993.

[Moo94]   I. Moon. Modeling programmable logic controllers for logic verification. *IEEE Control Systems*, 14(2):53–59, 1994.

[MS92]   K. L. McMillan and J. Schwalbe. Formal verification of the Gigamax cache consistency protocol. In *Proc. Int. Symp. on Shared Memory Multiprocessors, Tokyo, Japan, Apr. 1991*, pages 242–251. MIT Press, 1992.

[WV95]   J. M. Wing and M. Vaziri-Farahani. Model checking software systems: A case study. In *Proc. 3rd ACM SIGSOFT Symp. Foundations of Software Engineering (FSE'95), Washington, DC, USA, Oct. 1995*, pages 128–139, 1995.

13. SPIN – Communicating Automata

SPIN is a tool mainly developed by G. J. Holzmann at Bell Labs, Murray Hill, New Jersey, USA. SPIN was designed for simulation and verification of distributed algorithms. It is freely available via Internet [1].

13.1 What Can We Do with Spin?

The systems under study first have to be described in Promela, SPIN's specification language. Promela is an imperative language which looks like C augmented with a few communication primitives. Hence, Promela allows to describe the behavior of each process in the system, as well as the interactions between them. For communication, the processes may use *FIFO* (first in first out) communication channels, rendez-vous or shared variables.

SPIN essentially operates with two modes. The first one allows the user to get familiar with the behavior of his system by simulating its execution. The second one checks, by means of an exhaustive search of the set of reachable states, that the system satisfies some properties stated in e.g. PLTL, linear time temporal logic.

13.2 Spin's Essentials

The theoretical basis for SPIN originates from the model of automata communicating via *bounded* channels. SPIN does not permit to study infinite state systems (timed systems, Petri nets, etc.).

Its key feature is the availability of several state space reduction methods: state compression, on-the-fly verification and hashing techniques (via a *bit-state*, see below). Although finite, the number of reachable states of the systems modeled can easily reach tenth of millions !

Conclusion. SPIN is very simple to use and matches extremely well the needs for an introduction to problems inherent to verification of distributed systems. As for its performances, it provides a lot of new techniques to cope with state space explosion (intrinsic to verification of parallel systems).

---

[1] See http://netlib.bell-labs.com/netlib/spin/whatispin.html.

13.3 Describing Processes

The elevator example. The description of a system in Promela starts with constants definitions and global variables declarations. These global variables can be accessed by all processes, and therefore they are the *shared memory* of the system.

Consider again the small elevator with three floors. We start with the following declarations:

```
bit doorisopen[3];
chan openclosedoor=[0] of {byte,bit};
```

The bits array `doorisopen` indicates for the door of each floor whether it is open (1) or closed (0). The `openclosedoor` channel provides communication means between the elevator and the floor doors. The declaration states that the associated buffer has length 0, i.e. that the communication will be a rendez-vous. Moreover, the messages exchanged contain a byte (number of the floor to which the operation applies) and a bit (order sent to the door: 1 to open, 0 to close).

Each process starts with the keyword `proctype` followed by its name and its (possibly empty) list of arguments.

For example, process `door` takes a floor number as a parameter. It waits for an order to open, indicates that the door is open, and then that it is closed. Afterwards it signals the closing to the elevator:

```
proctype door(byte i){
do
:: openclosedoor?eval(i),1;
   doorisopen[i-1]=1;
   doorisopen[i-1]=0;
   openclosedoor!i,0
od
}
```

The classical instructions for changing the control flow are available to describe a process. The `do` loop which is used here is an infinite loop in which a non-deterministic choice is made between all instructions sequences starting with "::" (there is only one in the door process).

More generally, Promela's do...od provides a form of *guarded commands* in a CSP-like manner, where guards restrict the set of sequences that can be chosen.

This mechanism is used to control the elevator process:

```
proctype elevator(){
show byte floor = 1;

do
:: (floor != 3) -> floor++
:: (floor != 1) -> floor--
:: openclosedoor!floor,1;
   openclosedoor?eval(floor),0
od
}
```

This process contains two guards: (floor != 3) and (floor != 1) which check that the elevator is not at the top floor when going up nor at the bottom floor when going down. The third operation which can be performed by the elevator is to send an order to open to the door of the current floor. It then has to wait for the same door to close before moving.

The next step consists in joining all these parts. The system execution starts with an initialization process init:

```
init{
atomic{
run door(1); run door(2); run door(3);
run elevator()}
}
```

The instructions run door(1)... instantiate the processes corresponding to the three doors and the elevator. Each instance of the processes then runs in parallel with the ones that already exist.

13.4 Simulating the System

SPIN provides a simulation mode which allows the user to try out some executions with a nice and simple graphical user interface. Three simulation modes are available.

random: at each encounter of a non-deterministic choice, SPIN randomly chooses one of the possibilities ;
interactive: the user clicks on one of the executable instructions ;
guided: this mode is used together with verification (see section 13.5). When SPIN finds an error, it keeps a trace of the execution leading to this error, which can be replayed later in order to figure out the cause.

In any simulation mode, when performing a step by step simulation, SPIN allows the user to see the evolution of the system variables (or part of them). It

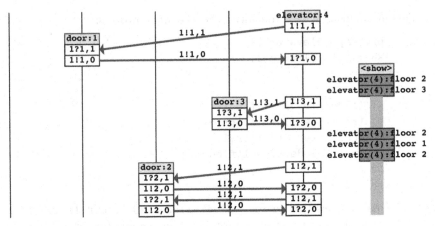

Fig. 13.1. Message Sequence Chart in SPIN simulation

is also possible to visualize the current instruction of each process. Figure 13.1 represents one of the possible synthetic views given by SPIN for an execution of our example. During this execution, the elevator process instructs the first floor door to open and then receives the door closure signal. When the door is closed, the elevator goes up to the second and third floor where it asks for the door to open, etc.

Simulation produces a view of the system functioning, but is not enough for an exhaustive verification. Therefore, we next proceed with a formal verification step.

13.5 Verification

The verification techniques proposed in SPIN consist in an analysis of the complete system. In particular, it allows one to check that some property is satisfied by all the reachable states or all the possible executions of the system.

SPIN provides a primitive to indicate invariants which should be satisfied when the system is in a given state. Thus, we can specify that when a door is open, both others should be closed, by adding the following assertion:

```
assert(doorisopen[i-1] &&
       !doorisopen[i%3] && !doorisopen[(i+1)%3]);
```

between the instructions to open and close door number i.

PLTL *model checking*. In SPIN, properties are specified as linear temporal logic formula. For example, we can prove that when the first floor door is open, it will necessarily be closed in the following state. This property can be written as a PLTL formula: $G(\text{open}_1 \Rightarrow X \text{ closed}_1)$. With SPIN, the formula is written:

```
[] (open1 -> X closed1)
```

where the corresponding atomic propositions are defined by:

```
#define open1 doorisopen[0]
#define closed1 !doorisopen[0]
```

SPIN then checks whether this formula is satisfied or not.

When the property is violated, SPIN keeps track of a counter-example execution, which can be replayed (see *guided* simulation section 13.4).

For example, consider the following property: $F(open_1 \vee open_2 \vee open_3)$, which means "eventually one of the three doors will be open", written:

```
<> (open1 || open2 || open3)

#define open1 doorisopen[0]
#define open2 doorisopen[1]
#define open3 doorisopen[2]
```

SPIN diagnostic indicates that the property is not satisfied and offers to replay a violating sequence. The simulation shows that our elevator can go up and down without ever stopping.

SPIN also provides other verifications, such as useless code detection, finding terminal states and *undesirable states*.

The bit-state *technique.* This method is one of the special features of SPIN. The *bit-state* method should be used when the amount of memory available is not large enough to perform an exhaustive search. The exhaustive verification algorithm used in SPIN to compute the set of all reachable states is a classical depth first search algorithm. The set of states already encountered is stored in a hash table with collision lists: these require to store all (or almost all) the information concerning a state, in order to check whether two states are identical or not.

The *bit-state* algorithm is similar to the classical one, but without collision list: all the available memory is used for the hash table. A state of the system is then identified by its hash key, and only one bit per state is needed, to indicate whether the state has already been encountered or not. The size of the hash table is then very large and collisions are unlikely to happen. In case two states collide (share the same hash table entry), they are merged (which can be seen as a folding of the reachability graph) and only the successors of only one of these states will be examined.

Thus, this technique leads to a partial search in the reachability graph. It allows one to find errors (it is always possible to check later on that a given execution is sensible), but it does not guarantee the validity of the system [2]. For example, this technique is particularly well-suited to the detection of undesired loops. In practice, it makes it possible to check many more states (by hundreds) than an exhaustive verification.

---

[2] In fact, we are not in one of the abstraction situations listed in chapter 11.

Let us finally mention that SPIN uses partial order reduction techniques to optimize its verifications.

13.6 Documentation and Case Studies

SPIN distribution includes a pedagogical manual, *Basic Spin Manual*, as well as several short examples. The reference is [Hol91], available on the Internet. It consists in a general discussion on communication protocols and their verification as well as the explanation of the theoretical concepts used in SPIN.

SPIN is widely used and has been the topic of an annual workshop since 1995. Case studies and enhancements are discussed there. The papers published in these workshops are available on the tool web pages, e.g.:

- [LS97], transcription in Promela of the steam boiler informal specification (this is a classical problem in specification). This paper also proposes a Promela compiler;
- [RL97], verification of part of a protocol that can be used to manage cars in the future (radio, telephone, GPS, ...);
- [JLS96], comparison and use of SPIN and UPPAAL to study a communication protocol without collisions between stations on a same bus.

Spin Bibliography

[Hol91] G. J. Holzmann. *Design and Validation of Computer Protocols.* Prentice Hall Int., 1991.

[JLS96] H. E. Jensen, K. G. Larsen, and A. Skou. Modelling and analysis of a collision avoidance protocol using SPIN and UPPAAL. In *Proc. 2nd SPIN Workshop, Rutgers, Piscataway, NJ, USA, Aug. 1996.* American Mathematical Society, 1996.

[LS97] S. Loeffler and A. Serhouchni. Creating a validated implementation of the Steam Boiler control. In *Proc. 3rd SPIN Workshop, Enschede, NL, Apr. 1997*, 1997.

[RL97] T. Ruys and R. Langerak. Validation of Bosch' mobile communication network architecture with SPIN. In *Proc. 3rd SPIN Workshop, Enschede, NL, Apr. 1997*, 1997.

14. DESIGN/CPN – Coloured Petri Nets

DESIGN/CPN was initially developed by *Meta Software Corp.*, Cambridge MA, USA, and the CPN· *Group* at the University of Århus, Denmark. Now, distributed and maintained by the CPN *Group*, the tool is free of charge and used by more than six hundred organizations, (a hundred of which are industrial) in fifty countries. It is available on the Internet [1].

14.1 What Can We Do with Design/CPN?

DESIGN/CPN allows one to edit, simulate and verify large hierarchical coloured Petri nets [2].

Both the editor and the simulator have a user-friendly graphical interface.

Verification is based on the (complete or partial) occurrence graph calculus. The user can provide a halting criterion when generating the occurrence graph, which may be infinite. It is then possible to formulate standard requests for properties such as reachability, deadlock, liveness as well as user-defined requests using the ML language [3].

14.2 Design/CPN's Essentials

DESIGN/CPN is the main tool for editing and analyzing coloured Petri nets. It is advertised a lot, by tool demonstrations during conferences, in the literature (Jensen in particular wrote three key books [Jen97a, Jen97b, Jen97c]), and also at the url mentioned above. Its web server is very complete.

With DESIGN/CPN, the description of large systems is made easier by the hierarchical constructs proposed. DESIGN/CPN also includes a notion of timed tokens.

Practical aspects are taken into account: the graphical interface is excellent for editing and simulating nets, DESIGN/CPN can provide statistical

---

[1] See http://www.daimi.au.dk/designCPN/.

[2] This presentation of DESIGN/CPN assumes minimal knowledge of Petri nets and their coloured extensions.

[3] In fact, it is an extension of the ML language which also provides simple access to the net components (places, transitions, ...)

reports as graphical output, it is based on the ML language and allows the user to improve the tool by writing ML libraries adapted to his own needs.

Most of the techniques used are standard. The occurrence graph can mainly be examined using *ad hoc* procedures. Compared to the other tools presented in this book, DESIGN/CPN did not integrate the last theoretical results in model checking, semantics of timed systems, etc.

Conclusion. DESIGN/CPN is an industrial size tool. It makes it possible to design quite easily very complex nets. During the simulations, the user can see the net execution directly on the graphical interface. The analyzing capabilities are a bit limited. A few extension libraries are available on DE-SIGN/CPN's web site. A user with a good experience of the ML programming language also has the opportunity to add his own features and libraries.

14.3 Editing with Design/CPN

```
val n = 5;
color PH = index ph with 1..n   declare ms;
color CS = index cs with 1..n   declare ms;
var p : PH;
fun Chopsticks(ph(i)) = 1'cs(i)+1'cs(if i=n then 1 else i+1);
```

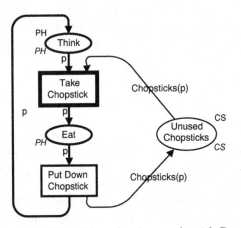

Fig. 14.1. The philosophers' example with DESIGN/CPN

Figure 14.1 shows the description of a net as a drawing, together with a box containing several declarations: constants, types (color sets), variables and functions in ML.

The example considered is a classical mutual exclusion problem: n Chinese philosophers (here $n = 5$), sitting around a table, can either eat or think. There is one chopstick between each pair of neighboring philosophers. A philosopher needs both his left and right chopsticks in order to be able to eat. Therefore his two neighbors must be thinking. With Coloured Petri nets, a unique net is needed to describe the behavior of the n philosophers, which are represented by n different colors.

In our example, this system is described as follows:

- PH is a set of colors $\{\text{ph}(1),\text{ph}(2),\text{ph}(3),\text{ph}(4),\text{ph}(5)\}$, i.e. one color per philosopher. Similarly, CS is the set of colors corresponding to the 5 chopsticks ;

- places Think and Eat have color set PH, and place Unused Chopsticks has color set CS ;

- the initial marking of place Think is the multi-set

  PH = 1'ph(1)+1'ph(2)+1'ph(3)+1'ph(4)+1'ph(5)

  which contains a copy of each philosopher. This multi-set is defined in the declarations by the keyword declare ms. Place Eat is initially empty. The initial marking of place Unused Chopsticks is the multi-set

  CS = 1'cs(1)+1'cs(2)+1'cs(3)+1'cs(4)+1'cs(5);

- The transition firing conditions and their results are indicated by the arc inscriptions. For example, transition Take Chopstick takes as input a philosopher p from place Think, and his two chopsticks from place Unused Chopsticks. Function Chopsticks, defined in ML by fun Chopsticks(ph(i)) = ..., associates each philosopher with the two chopsticks he needs.

Since the description of a net is quite technical, close to programming, a syntactical net checker is provided. The drawing itself is done using the mouse to select, in pull-down menus of the main window, options for the creation of places, transitions and arcs.

The modular and hierarchical aspects of the design of systems is particularly well handled. Systems may be built using either a bottom-up or a top-down approach.

14.4 Simulating the Net

Once the net has been described and compiled, the user can enter the simulation mode. Simulations can be interactive or automatic.

Interactive simulations. Firable transitions are highlighted on the drawing: their border is thicker and in a different color. The user chooses a transition and asks the system for one (or more) *binding* (i.e., values for the different variables involved in the firing of the transition). When the binding is chosen, the transition is fired and the graphics updated.

In the example of the philosophers, `Take Chopstick` is the only firable transition. When it is selected, five bindings are possible, since five different philosophers can be assigned to the variable p that appears both on the arc from `Think` to `Take Chopstick`, and as a parameter of function `Chopsticks` on the arc from `Unused Chopsticks` to `Take Chopstick`.

Automatic simulation. Transitions are fired at random. Simulation can be performed with or without halting criteria. The user can set halting criteria of two kinds:

- a given number of steps;
- a time limit after which the execution stops.

The second criterion is valid for timed nets. In this context, the firing rule is the following. A global clock is started. Tokens are stamped with a date at which they can be used (they are said to be *ready*). The arc expressions from a transition to a place carry a *temporal clause* called a *delay*. When a token is created, its time stamp is the value of the global clock plus the delay. The global clock is incremented when no token is ready. This way of introducing time in nets ensures that a token will remain for some time in a place.

Simulation reports. The default simulation report of DESIGN/CPN is short: it is a piece of text (saved in a file) composed of the list of transitions fired together with the associated bindings.

However, DESIGN/CPN allows one to obtain personalized simulation reports, using *code segments*. An ML procedure can be associated with each transition. It will be executed each time the transition is fired. The binding associated with the transition fired can be found using the keyword `input`. When using code segments, one can obtain his own format of simulation report as well as graphic updates. However, this method requires a good knowledge of ML.

In the example of the philosophers, it would be possible to generate a bar chart showing how many times each philosopher ate during a simulation. To do so, we can associate the following code segment with transition `Take Chopstick`:

```
input(p);
action
    updateEat(p);
```

and define function `updateEat` as:

```
val numberEat = ref(Array.array(n,0));
fun updateEat(ph(i)) =
        Array.update(!numberEat,i,Array.sub(!numberEat,i)+1);
```

14.5 Analyzing the Net

Occurrence graph. The *Occurrence Graph Tool* is used for analyzing the net. It constructs the reachability graph in which the nodes are global states of the system, and the oriented arcs indicate how to go from one state to another. Nowadays the tool can handle graphs with up to 200,000 states and 2,000,000 arcs. The generation is done with either breadth first or depth first search.

The simulator and the occurrence graph tool are very close and can be used together. It is indeed possible to transfer a state from the occurrence graph into the simulator and vice-versa.

Placing nodes of the occurrence graph on the graphical output must be done manually. The system displays the nodes (and the arcs to their neighbors) and the user places the nodes in the window with the mouse. The user can decide to see the particular nodes he is interested in, the markings, and the arc labels. Figure 14.2 shows the reachability graph for the philosophers (in which we explicitly asked to see four arc labels and three markings). Here the graph is small and thus fully displayed.

The graph may be infinite, and thus the user must provide the tool with a set of halting criteria which can be, for instance the size of the graph or more elaborate ones written in ML : for example, stop building the graph as soon as a deadlock is encountered.

In order to alleviate the state explosion problem, the user can specify, in ML, equivalences between markings and between transitions with bindings [Jen97b]. The *OE/OS Graph Tool* generates an occurrence graph modulo these equivalences. The graph thus obtained can be analyzed, like the standard occurrence graph. The results depend on the equivalence used (permutations, symmetries, ...)

Verification. The user can ask for the generation of a standard report that gives basic information about: statistics (size of the graph and computation time), *boundedness, home states, deadlocks, liveness* and *fairness*. However if the graph was partially generated, these answers to verification problems are also partial, e.g. if there is a deadlock, the net is not live, but if there is no deadlock in the partial graph, nothing can be deduced.

Several libraries exist which are regularly updated. In particular, it is possible to write CTL requests.

14.6 Documentation and Case Studies

DESIGN/CPN web server provides a very clear and exhaustive manual as well as a tutorial. All the examples presented in [Jen97a, Jen97b, Jen97c] agree with the syntax and features of the tool.

The third volume of Jensen's *Coloured Petri Nets* series [Jen97c] is entirely dedicated to practical applications of coloured nets using DESIGN/CPN. Some examples are:

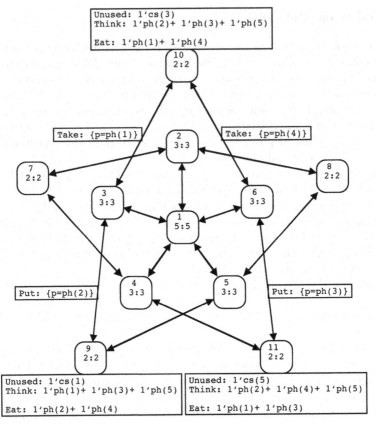

Fig. 14.2. Occurrence graph of the philosophers' example with DESIGN/CPN

- audio/video system: project by Bang & Olufsen A/S (Denmark) and Århus university [CJ97] ;
- electronic funds transfer: project between the Société Générale, Marine Midland Bank of New York and Meta Software [PS91] ;
- command and control of a naval vessel: project accomplished by the Defense Research Establishment Valcartier (Québec) [BL93] ;
- *Usage Parameter Control* of ATM networks: project done by Århus university [CJ93] ;
- several industrial applications which have been presented at the CPN [Jen98, Jen99] and HLPN [Jen00] workshops.

Design/CPN Bibliography

[BL93] J. Berger and L. Lamontagne. A colored Petri net model for a naval command and control system. In *Proc. 14th Int. Conf. Application and Theory of Petri Nets (ICATPN'93), Chicago, IL, USA, June 1993*, volume 691 of *Lecture Notes in Computer Science*, pages 532–541. Springer, 1993.

[CJ93]   H. Clausen and P. R. Jensen. Validation and performance analysis of network algorithms by coloured Petri nets. In *Proc. 5th Int. Workshop on Petri Nets and Performance Models (PNPM'93), Toulouse, France, 1993*, pages 280–289. IEEE Comp. Soc. Press, 1993.

[CJ97]   S. Christensen and J. B. Jørgensen. Analysing Bang & Olufsen's BeoLink audio/video system using coloured Petri nets. In *Proc. 18th Int. Conf. Application and Theory of Petri Nets (ICATPN'97), Toulouse, France, June 1997*, volume 1248 of *Lecture Notes in Computer Science*, pages 387–406. Springer, 1997.

[Jen97a] K. Jensen. *Coloured Petri Nets. Basic Concepts, Analysis Methods and Practical Use. Vol. 1, Basic Concepts.* EATCS Monographs in Theoretical Computer Science. Springer, 1997. 2nd ed., 2nd corr. printing.

[Jen97b] K. Jensen. *Coloured Petri Nets. Basic Concepts, Analysis Methods and Practical Use. Vol. 2, Analysis Methods.* EATCS Monographs in Theoretical Computer Science. Springer, 1997. 2nd corr. printing.

[Jen97c] K. Jensen. *Coloured Petri Nets. Basic Concepts, Analysis Methods and Practical Use. Vol. 3, Practical Use.* EATCS Monographs in Theoretical Computer Science. Springer, 1997.

[Jen98]   K. Jensen, editor. *Proceedings of the CPN Workshop (CPN'98), Aarhus, DK, June 1998*, 1998. Available at `http://www.daimi.au.dk/CPnets/workshop98`.

[Jen99]   K. Jensen, editor. *Proceedings of the CPN Workshop (CPN'99), Aarhus, DK, October 1999*, 1999. Available at `http://www.daimi.au.dk/CPnets/workshop99`.

[Jen00]   K. Jensen, editor. *Proceedings of Workshop on Practical use of High-Level Petri Nets (HLPN'00), Aarhus, DK*, 2000. Available at `http://www.daimi.au.dk/pn2000/proceedings/`.

[PS91]   V. O. Pinci and R. M. Shapiro. An integrated software development methodology based on hierarchical coloured Petri nets. In *Advances in Petri Nets 1991*, volume 524 of *Lecture Notes in Computer Science*, pages 649–667. Springer, 1991.

15. UPPAAL – Timed Systems

UPPAAL is being developed jointly by the Basic Research in Computer Science laboratory at Aalborg University in Denmark and the Department of Computer Systems at Uppsala University in Sweden, mainly by W. Yi, K. G. Larsen and P. Pettersson. UPPAAL is an integrated tool environment for modeling, simulating and verifying real-time systems. It is freely available (for non-profit applications) on the Internet [1].

15.1 What Can We Do with Uppaal?

UPPAAL allows one to analyze networks of timed automata with binary synchronization. It contains three main parts. First, timed processes are described using a *graphical editor*. Second, systems can be simulated, viz. we can choose to perform a sequence of transitions, and have a look at the behavior of the designed system. This is done by a *graphical simulator*. Finally reachability properties can be verified (for example "is it possible to reach a state where clock x is greater than 5?", or "is it true that for any reachable configuration, when the train is on the crossing, the gate is closed?"). This is done by *the verifier*.

15.2 Uppaal's Essentials

The friendly graphical user interface makes UPPAAL an excellent tool for modeling and verifying real-time systems.

The main drawbacks of UPPAAL are linked to the modeling formalism. First, binary synchronization is a bit restrictive and requires one to use *ad hoc* mechanisms to describe other kinds of synchronizations (e.g., broadcast). Second, the specification language considers only reachability properties and not a full temporal logic; this entails that testing (or observer) automata are required (section 11.6) to express complex properties.

---

[1] See http://www.uppaal.com/.

Conclusion. UPPAAL is a very pleasant tool to analyze timed systems. Note that even though verification is difficult for very big systems due to complexity reasons, simulation is always possible and gives very useful hints about the system under study.

15.3 Modeling Timed Systems with Uppaal

Since September 1999 (version UPPAAL2k), the tool has had its own graphical system editor which allows one to easily draw networks of timed automata. Note that it is also possible to use a textual format to describe systems.

The main differences between timed processes used by UPPAAL and classical timed automata of section 5 are integer variables, which are permitted in UPPAAL systems and synchronization between timed processes.

Integer variables. It is possible to use integer variables in the description of timed systems in UPPAAL. This makes the modeling process of complex systems easier (see section 1.4). Note that such integer variables and the clocks can be global to the whole system or local to a process; they can be used in guards of transitions, in the invariant constraints and they can be updated when a transition is performed.

Synchronization. In UPPAAL, timed automata can communicate using a binary synchronization function based on the classical message passing model (see section 1.5). Given a communication channel a, an action a! (sending on channel a) and an action a? (receiving on channel a) have to be performed synchronously. This mechanism is restrictive and, for example, does not allow for broadcast but this can be modeled by *ad hoc* constructions (e.g. committed locations).

Some channels can be defined as *urgent channels*: when a transition on such a channel a is possible (i.e. when an action a! and an action a? can be performed by two timed automata), no delay transition is enabled as long as an urgent communication is possible. Along the same line, urgent control states exist: when the current state of an automaton has been defined as *urgent location*, no delay transition is allowed as long as there is a urgent location in the configuration.

Finally, a control state can be defined as *committed location*: if the current configuration of the network contains such a control state, only (action) transitions leaving this state are possible (in particular no delay transition is possible). A broadcast and more generally any *n*-ary synchronization can be simulated by using such committed locations.

New features in UPPAAL*2k.* Bounded integer variables (or arrays of them) can be defined. Timed processes can be designed by using templates with parameters. Given such a template, several timed processes can be defined. This is very useful for systems with several identical components.

Train crossing example. This system (see section 5.2) can be modeled in
UPPAAL as a network of timed automata described in Figures 15.1, 15.2
and 15.3. The integer variable C in the controller process is used to count
the number of trains moving between the signals *App* and *Exit*. Then, the
current system can easily be extended to any number of trains.

The textual description of a system starts with the definition of global
clocks, global integer variables and channels. For the railway crossing example, only the channels are global:

```
chan  app, exit, GoDown, GoUp;      // Channels
```

The textual description of the train's template is:

```
process Train{
    clock x;
    state far, near{x<30}, on{x<20};
    init far;
    trans near -> on {
            guard x>20, x<30;
            assign x:=0;
        },
        far -> near {
            sync App!;
            assign x:=0;
        },
        on -> far {
            guard x>10, x<20;
            sync Exit!;
        };
}
```

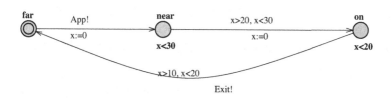

Fig. 15.1. A template for train processes

The definition of a template for trains starts with the list of control states
followed by their invariant between braces if any (it is **true** by default). Then
the list of transitions is given. For any transition, we have the source state
and the target state, and three additional components may appear: the guard

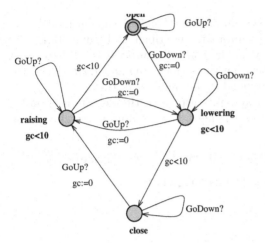

Fig. 15.2. The gate

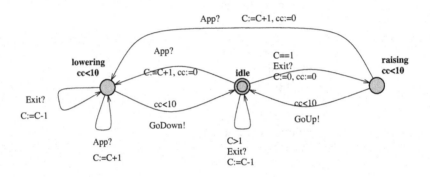

Fig. 15.3. The controller

of the transition, the synchronization action (a channel name followed by !
or ?) and an update action over variables and clocks. From this template, we
define several timed processes corresponding to several trains in the model:

```
Train1:=Train();
Train2:=Train();
Train3:=Train();
```

Finally the network is defined by an instruction of the form:

```
system Train1, Train2, Train3, Gate, Controller
```

Figures 15.1, 15.2 and 15.3 have been produced directly form the graphical
editor of version 3.0.41 of UPPAAL2k.

15.4 Simulating a System

Simulating is very useful to validate the model: it allows one to verify on simple cases that the behavior of the model meets its specification. Clearly the *graphical simulator* of UPPAAL is an important help for designing complex systems.

Executions of a system can be investigated in a dynamic way with the simulator. We can select transitions step-by-step, have a look on the value of variables and clocks, save executions ... Moreover it is possible to fire transitions in a random manner: we fix the length of the run and the speed of the simulation, and (at any step) an enabled transition is randomly selected and performed. This gives an overview of the behavior of the system. Finally it is possible to get diagnostic traces from the model checking module and such traces can be played within the simulator.

Note that simulating is not verifying: simulation does not consider the exhaustive behavior of the system; therefore no safety proof can be given after this step (only a model-checker can prove safety properties), but it often enables one to find bugs in a model, correct it and validate it.

15.5 Verification

The third part of UPPAAL is the verifier. It implements model checking for reachability properties over networks of timed automata. Atomic propositions are basic constraints over control locations of the system and the values of clocks and variables:

- S.r expresses that the current location of automaton S is r ;
- t $\sim$ n expresses that the current value of t satisfies the test where t denotes a global or local variable (or clock), $n \in \mathbb{N}$ and $\sim \in \{=, <, >, \leq, \geq\}$.

Given a boolean combination P built from not, and, or and imply operators and atomic propositions, there are two kinds of reachability properties based on operators AG and EF of CTL temporal logic:

- AGP : " P holds for any reachable configuration" is written A[]P in UPPAAL format. For example, in the train crossing, the property "when a train is on the crossing, the gate is down" is expressed with the following formula:

    A[] ((Train1.on or Train2.on or Train3.on) imply Gate.close)

- EFP : "It is possible to reach a configuration verifying P" is written E<>P in UPPAAL.

    Note that nesting operators EF and AG is not allowed.

    Remember that the answer given by the model checker deals with all possible executions: it produces an exhaustive analysis of the behavior of the system. Of course when the property studied is of the form E<>P, the verifier stops as soon as it finds a configuration C verifying P ; moreover it gives a *diagnostic trace* leading to C. If the property is of the form A[]P, UPPAAL needs to consider every reachable configuration except if it finds one for which P does not hold; in this case, the program stops and gives a diagnostic trace leading to this configuration.

Different options are available to tune the reachability algorithm: breadth-first or depth-first search, reductions to save memory space ... Anyway the theoretical complexity is very high (see section 5.5) and it is sometimes impossible to get an answer for a query if the decision procedure requires to visit too many reachable configurations. Note that this restriction does not hold for simulation: it is always possible, even for a big system. Using the verifier successfully depends a lot on the size of the input model and especially on the number of clocks. If verification is not feasible, the model has to be simplified by abstraction as described in section 11.6.

The specification language used for the verifier is too restricted, it contains only simple reachability properties. In the train crossing example, it would be interesting to express that "the gate is open at most 70 seconds after an exit signal if no train approaches the railroad crossing in between". To verify such a property we need to use the testing automata technique (see section 11.6).

15.6 Documentation and Case Studies

The paper "UPPAAL in a Nutshell" [LPY97] available on the web server of UPPAAL is a good introduction to this tool. However it deals with the previous version based on an old graphical editor and some features were not yet available. Today, no complete document exists for the new version UPPAAL2k but small presentations can be found on the server and the tool is delivered with demo examples.

Many applications have been modeled and verified with UPPAAL, among which we can mention:

- audio-video protocol of Bang & Olufsen [HSLL97, HLS99] ;
- audio control protocol of Philips [BGK+96] ;
- analysis of a gear controller [LPY98] ;
- verification of a TDMA protocol [LP97].

Uppaal Bibliography

[BGK+96] J. Bengtsson, W. O. D. Griffioen, K. J. Kristoffersen, K. G. Larsen, F. Larsson, P. Pettersson, and Wang Yi. Verification of an audio protocol with bus collision using UPPAAL. In *Proc. 8th Int. Conf. Computer Aided Verification (CAV'96), New Brunswick, NJ, USA, July-Aug.*

1996, volume 1102 of *Lecture Notes in Computer Science*, pages 244–256. Springer, 1996.

[HLS99] K. Havelund, K. G. Larsen, and A. Skou. Formal verification of a power controller using the real-time model checker UPPAAL. In *Proc. 5th Int. AMAST Workshop Formal Methods for Real-Time and Probabilistic Systems (ARTS'99), Bamberg, Germany, May 1999*, volume 1601 of *Lecture Notes in Computer Science*, pages 277–298. Springer, 1999.

[HSLL97] K. Havelund, A. Skou, K. G. Larsen, and K. Lund. Formal modelling and analysis of an audio/video protocol: An industrial case study using UP-PAAL. In *Proc. 18th IEEE Real-Time Systems Symposium (RTSS'97), San Francisco, CA, USA, Dec. 1997*, pages 2–13. IEEE Comp. Soc. Press, 1997.

[LP97] H. Lönn and P. Pettersson. Formal verification of a TDMA protocol start-up mechanism. In *Proc. IEEE Pacific Rim Int. Symp. on Fault-Tolerant Systems, Taipei, Taiwan, Dec. 1997*, pages 235–242, 1997.

[LPY97] K. G. Larsen, P. Pettersson, and Wang Yi. UPPAAL in a nutshell. *Journal of Software Tools for Technology Transfer*, 1(1–2):134–152, 1997.

[LPY98] M. Lindahl, P. Pettersson, and Wang Yi. Formal design and analysis of a gear controller. In *Proc. 4th Int. Conf. Tools and Algorithms for the Construction and Analysis of Systems (TACAS'98), Lisbon, Portugal, March 1998*, volume 1384 of *Lecture Notes in Computer Science*, pages 281–297. Springer, 1998.

16. KRONOS – Model Checking of Real-time Systems

KRONOS allows us to analyze timed automata. It is developed at VERIMAG [1] by S. Yovine, A. Olivero, C. Daws and S. Tripakis, and is available on the Internet [2].

16.1 What Can We Do with Kronos?

KRONOS is a model checker for the TCTL logic (see chapter 5): it can decide whether some property, expressed by a TCTL formula, holds for a timed automaton (also called timed graph), given in textual form. starting from a system consisting of several components, KRONOS computes the automaton corresponding to the synchronized product.

16.2 Kronos' Essentials

1. KRONOS is one of the very few tools which implements a model checking algorithm for a timed temporal logic. For this reason, it allows one to verify liveness properties, and is not restricted to reachability properties like UPPAAL and HYTECH.

2. Besides the usual limits on the size of systems, which are particularly drastic for timed models, KRONOS contains no graphical nor simulation modes. Some of its design features can also seem strange at first sight.

Conclusion. KRONOS is a true timed model checker, with noticeable performances. However, under its current form, it is mostly intended for advanced users, with a good knowledge of formal methods.

---

[1] University of Grenoble and CNRS.
[2] See http://www-verimag.imag.fr/TEMPORISE/kronos.

16.3 Describing Automata

The railroad crossing example from chapter 5 can be represented by a system with two trains, a gate, a controller and a counter[3], used to detect the last train going out from the crossing.

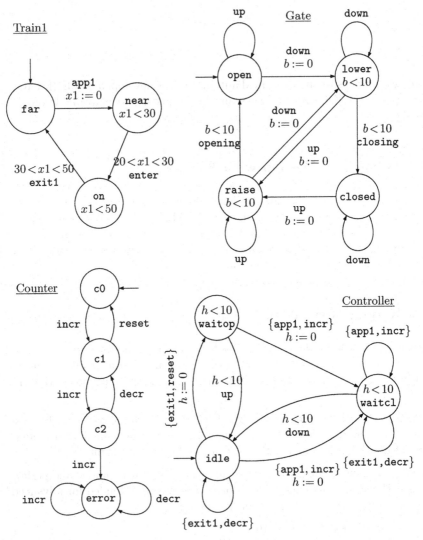

Fig. 16.1. A railway crossing model

---

[3] This counter plays the same role as the integer variable c used by UPPAAL in chapter 15.

In order to illustrate this system in a more readable manner, figure 16.1
contains a single train. Moreover, in the automaton of the controller, we chose
to omit the six transitions needed for the synchronization with the second
train. Of course these transitions are simple copies of the ones used for the
synchronization between the controller and the first train. Note that each
automaton must be defined in a separate file (with extension .tg meaning
"timed graph"). The textual description of the automaton for the first train
is in file Tr1.tg:

```
/* train1 */
#locs 3
#trans 3
#clocks x1
#sync app1 exit1

loc: 0
prop: far
inv: TRUE
trans: TRUE => app1; x1:=0; goto 1

loc: 1
prop: near
inv: x1<30
trans: x1>20 and x1<30 => enter; ; goto 2

loc: 2
prop: on
inv: x1<50
trans: x1>20 and x1<50 => exit1; ; goto 0
```

The number of states and transitions, the clocks and the synchronization
labels are declared in the first lines. The control states must always be called
0, 1, etc., after loc:. For instance, loc: 1 describes the state where the
train approaches the crossing. An invariant is associated with each control
state, such as inv: x1<30 or inv: TRUE, as well as one or more atomic
propositions like prop: on and the transitions going out from this state.
Each such transition contains:

- a guard, for instance x1>10 and x1<20, or True when no condition is required for the firing of the transition;
- a label corresponding either to an internal action (enter), or a synchronization (exit1);
- possibly some clock resets (x1:=0);
- the target state (goto 2).

Labeling a state by the proposition init makes it an initial state. When the
proposition does not appear, state 0 is the initial state.

16.4 Synchronized Product

In order for several components of a system to communicate, KRONOS introduces a synchronization function which is not the most general, but includes the mechanisms proposed in both UPPAAL and HYTECH. Handling this technique is not easy at first and some training may prove useful.

In KRONOS, a transition is equipped with a non-empty *set* of labels, instead of a single (possibly fictitious) label in classical models. The main interest of this method is to avoid tuples of labels or renaming operations on them when building the transitions in a product automaton. In the case of KRONOS, a synchronization label is simply obtained by the union of the label sets of the components.

It remains to precisely define when transitions have to be synchronized. Intuitively, a set of transitions (from distinct components) are synchronized if and only if each label occurring in one of the transition sets also belongs to (at least) one set of another transition.

For example, if $\mathcal{A}_1$ contains the single transition t_1: $q_1 \xrightarrow{\{a,b\}} r_1$, if $\mathcal{A}_2$ contains the single transition t_2: $q_2 \xrightarrow{\{b,c\}} r_2$, and if b is a synchronization label, then the product of automata $\mathcal{A}_1$ and $\mathcal{A}_2$ contains transition $q_1q_2 \xrightarrow{\{a,b,c\}} r_1r_2$.

On the contrary, transition $q_1q_2 \xrightarrow{\{a,b\}} r_1q_2$ cannot appear in the product. Otherwise t_1 should be synchronized with another transition t_2' of the form $q_2 \xrightarrow{\quad} q_2$ (see section 1.5), but this is impossible because t_1 contains synchronization labels that do not synchronize with any label in t_2'.

In the case of disjoint label sets, there is no transition synchronization for the standard product of KRONOS.

Although this definition may seem rather natural, the product thus obtained in KRONOS is not an associative operation, which turns out to be awkward for the design of systems.

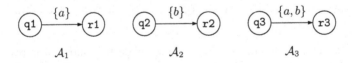

Fig. 16.2. Three simple automata

An example. Consider the three automata in figure 16.2. If we want to make first the product of $\mathcal{A}_1$ and $\mathcal{A}_2$, and then compose the result ($\mathcal{A}_{12}$) with $\mathcal{A}_3$, we have to write the following commands:

```
kronos -out A12.tg A1.tg A2.tg
kronos -out A12A3.tg A12.tg A3.tg
```

which produce files `A12.tg` and `A12A3.tg`. The latter file contains the description of the automaton $\mathcal{A}_{(12)3}$, which has no transition. If we now compute the product of $\mathcal{A}_1$ with the result $\mathcal{A}_{23}$ of composing $\mathcal{A}_2$ and $\mathcal{A}_3$, we obtain the product automaton $\mathcal{A}_{1(23)}$, which has exactly one transition labeled $\{a, b\}$! Unfortunately, it is not easy to use a modular approach with a non associative product.

There are two ways to overcome this problem. The first one consists in building in a single operation the product of all components of a given system. For instance, in the railroad crossing model, the command:

```
kronos -out S.tg Tr1.tg Tr2.tg Gate.tg Contr.tg Ct.tg
```

makes a syntactical verification of the component automata already defined (in `Tr1.tg`, `Tr2.tg`, etc.) and builds the product, described in file `S.tg`.

The second way uses a special option `-sd`, which asks KRONOS to add in the product the transitions with disjoint sets of labels. For instance, the command:

```
kronos -sd -out A12.tg A1.tg A2.tg
```

yields the automaton $\mathcal{A}'_{12}$, on the right of figure 16.3. In turn, this automaton will have a non-empty synchronization with $\mathcal{A}_3$ on label $\{a, b\}$.

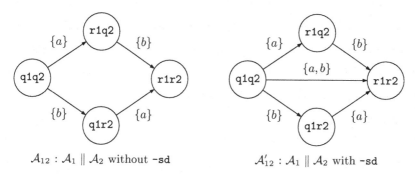

$\mathcal{A}_{12} : \mathcal{A}_1 \parallel \mathcal{A}_2$ without `-sd` $\mathcal{A}'_{12} : \mathcal{A}_1 \parallel \mathcal{A}_2$ with `-sd`

Fig. 16.3. Option `-sd` for synchronization

16.5 Model Checking

Now the properties to be checked must be expressed by TCTL formulas, each being in a separate file with extension `.tctl`.

A safety property. The (untimed) property: "when a train is inside the crossing, the gate is closed", is described in the file safe.tctl by the formula:

```
init impl AB(on impl closed)
```

In which impl is the boolean combinator $\Rightarrow$, while A and B correspond respectively to the classical untimed operators A and G of CTL.

Verifying this safety property is done with the KRONOS command:

```
kronos -back S.tg safe.tctl
```

The file safe.eval thus generated contains the result (**true**) obtained by a "backwards analysis" (the option -back stands for *backwards*). Note that a "forward" analysis of the same formula (the option -forw uses another model checking algorithm) fails because of the size of the problem.

A liveness property. The timed property $V(d)$, "from the moment where no train arrives anymore, the gate will finally be open after d time units", is expressed by the TCTL formula:

$$\text{init} \Rightarrow \mathsf{AG}(\neg\mathsf{near} \wedge \neg\mathsf{on} \Rightarrow \neg\mathsf{E}(\neg\mathsf{near} \wedge \neg\mathsf{on} \wedge \neg\mathsf{open})\mathsf{U}_{(>d)}\mathsf{true}))$$

written in KRONOS when $d = 20$:

```
init impl
AB((not near and not on) impl
   not((not near and not on and not open) EU{>20} TRUE))
```

KRONOS allows one to verify that the liveness property holds for $d = 20$: the resulting file V20.eval contains **true**.

```
kronos: begin evaluation of V20.tctl
kronos: end evaluation of V20.tctl
kronos: compacting
kronos: file V20.eval created

-----------------------------------------------------------------
kronos: fixpoint    : system 0.000s * user 0.030s * #iterations 5
kronos: compact time: system 0.000s * user 0.000s *
kronos: total time  : system 0.000s * user 0.050s *
-----------------------------------------------------------------
```

On the other hand, KRONOS finds that the property does not hold for $d = 19$. Evaluation of V19.tctl needs 13 iteration steps and produces the subset $Sat(V(19))$ (see section 4.1), which contains the system states satisfying the formula $V19$. We can conclude that the property is not true because this subset $Sat(V(19))$ is not equal to the set of all system states.

16.6 Documentation and Case Studies

The user guide is "Kronos User's Manual (Release 2.2)", available on the web page mentioned at the beginning. It contains 23 pages and shortly describes the model and analysis method. Textual descriptions of the automata and TCTL formulae are shown for a particular example: a collision problem for multiple communication through a bus. However, many syntactical details of KRONOS are missing and left for the reader to guess.

Several case studies with KRONOS are available, among which:

- numerous timed communication protocols: CSMA/CD [DOY94], Philips Audio-Control [DY95], CNET FRP-DT [TY98], FDDI [DT98];
- analysis of linear hybrid systems [OSY94], a robot in an automatic manufacturing plant [DY95] ;
- Fischer's mutual exclusion protocol [DT98] ;
- MOS circuits [BMPY97].

The model of timed graphs is proposed and studied in [ACD93, HMP94].

Kronos Bibliography

[ACD93]   R. Alur, C. Courcoubetis, and D. Dill. Model-checking in dense real-time. *Information and Computation*, 104(1):2–34, 1993.

[BMPY97] M. Bozga, O. Maler, A. Pnueli, and S. Yovine. Some progress in the symbolic verification of timed automata. In *Proc. 9th Int. Conf. Computer Aided Verification (CAV'97), Haifa, Israel, June 1997*, volume 1254 of *Lecture Notes in Computer Science*, pages 179–190. Springer, 1997.

[DOY94]   C. Daws, A. Olivero, and S. Yovine. Verifying ET-LOTOS programs with KRONOS. In *Proc. Formal Description Techniques (FORTE'94), Bern, Switzerland, Oct. 1994*, pages 227–242. Chapman & Hall, 1994.

[DT98]   C. Daws and S. Tripakis. Model-checking of real-time reachability properties using abstractions. In *Proc. 4th Int. Conf. Tools and Algorithms for the Construction and Analysis of Systems (TACAS'98), Lisbon, Portugal, March 1998*, volume 1384 of *Lecture Notes in Computer Science*, pages 313–329. Springer, 1998.

[DY95]   C. Daws and S. Yovine. Two examples of verification of multirate timed automata with KRONOS. In *Proc. 16th IEEE Real-Time Systems Symposium (RTSS'95), Pisa, Italy, Dec. 1995*, pages 66–75. IEEE Comp. Soc. Press, 1995.

[HMP94]   T. A. Henzinger, Z. Manna, and A. Pnueli. Temporal proof methodologies for timed transition systems. *Information and Computation*, 112(2):273–337, 1994.

[OSY94]   A. Olivero, J. Sifakis, and S. Yovine. Using abstractions for the verification of linear hybrid systems. In *Proc. 6th Int. Conf. Computer Aided Verification (CAV'94), Stanford, CA, USA, June 1994*, volume 818 of *Lecture Notes in Computer Science*, pages 81–94. Springer, 1994.

[TY98]   S. Tripakis and S. Yovine. Verification of the fast reservation protocol with delayed transmission using the tool Kronos. In *Proc. 4th IEEE Real-Time Technology and Applications Symposium (RTAS'98), Denver, CO, USA, June. 1998*. IEEE Comp. Soc. Press, 1998.

17. HYTECH – Linear Hybrid Systems

HYTECH allows one to analyze linear hybrid automata. It was developed by T. A. Henzinger, P.-H. Ho and H. Wong-Toi, at Cornell University, and improvements were added at the University of California, Berkeley, and is available on the Internet [1].

17.1 What Can We Do With HyTech?

A set of linear hybrid automata, synchronized by some common transitions, is given to HYTECH. [2] From the automata in a textual form, HYTECH can compute subsets of the global state space, when these subsets are described by expressions combining propositional constraints and accessibility properties. The result of this computation (its form, whether it is empty or not, etc.) gives information about the behavior of the system. HYTECH also handles parametric analysis (see section 17.5).

17.2 HyTech's Essentials

HYTECH is a very good tool for the analysis of linear hybrid systems, the only one handling parametric models. This is particularly useful for the design and verification of systems. Moreover, with the extended expressive power of linear hybrid systems, it is possible to describe seemingly distant models (like Petri nets for instance), to which this parametric analysis can be applied.

HYTECH has two main limitations:

1. This is an academic tool, including no simulation mode. Model checking does not apply to a temporal logic: the user has to build himself the subset of states to be computed, by combinations of basic constraints.
2. The size of the system to be analyzed is rather small, but complexity is an intrinsic limit of the model checking approach.

---

[1] See http://www.eecs.berkeley.edu/~tah/HyTech.

[2] Recall that most verification problems are undecidable in this framework, see section 5.3.

Conclusion. this is a useful and powerful tool, with no equivalent for the design and symbolic analysis of hybrid systems. Although not very attractive, it is rather easy to use and applies to a large class of systems.

17.3 Describing Automata

Variables. Linear hybrid automata are equipped with global variables, whose real values increase linearly with time. These variables are declared with their type at the beginning of the file containing the description of the system.

A variable can evolve in two different ways. A transition can change its value instantaneously. In a given state, its value increases continuously with time. The *slope* of a variable v, written dv, is its speed. For a *linear* hybrid automaton, this slope has a fixed value in the state between two transitions. A variable has the type discrete if its slope is 0 in any state and the type clock if its slope is 1. When the slope can change according to the different states, its type is called analog.

Synchronization. The synchronization function used in HyTech is simple: transitions from different automata must synchronize if they have the same label. It is a restricted mode of the general method described in chapter 1, in which particular sets Sync are used. All the tuples in Sync are of the form $(e_1, \ldots, e_n)$, where the e_i's are either the label e of a single action, or the special label -, corresponding to no action for a component which does not move.

The railroad crossing example. We consider the simplest version of this problem [3], in which the system consists only of a train and a gate, synchronized by signals app (for "approach"). Using HyTech, the gate can be modeled by a linear hybrid automaton with a variable a representing the angle of the gate. When a=90, the gate is completely open, while it is closed for a=0. This variable a and the clock x of the train are declared as follows:

```
var     a : analog;
        x : clock;
```

and the automaton is defined by:

```
automaton gate
synclabs: app, exit;
initially up & a=90;

loc up: while True wait {da=0}
        when True sync exit goto up;
        when True sync app goto lower;
```

---

[3] See chapter 5.

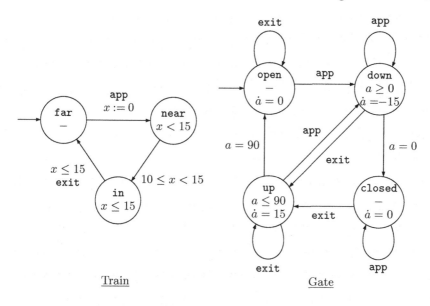

Fig. 17.1. Railway crossing linear hybrid automata

```
loc lower: while a>=0 wait {da=-15}
        when a=0 goto down;
        when True sync exit goto raise;
        when True sync app goto lower;

loc down: while True wait {da=0}
        when True sync exit goto raise;
        when True sync app goto down;

loc raise: while a<=90 wait {da=15}
        when a=90 goto up;
        when True sync exit goto raise;
        when True sync app goto lower;

    end -- gate
```

The name of a control state in an automaton is preceded by `loc`, as in `loc raise:`, which describes the state where the gate is opening. Three elements are associated with a control state:

- an invariant is a condition on variables which must hold in this state, for instance `while a<=90` or `while True`;
- the slope of the variables is described by their derivative, written `da` for variable a, with values following `wait`, as in `wait {da=15}` or `wait {da=0}`. It is also possible to use an interval: `wait {da in [5, 8]}` ;

- the transitions going out of the state contain:
  1. a guard: **when a=90**, or **when True** when no firing condition is required, or also **asap**, for " as soon as possible ", when a transition is urgent .
  2. Possibly a synchronization label: **sync exit**.
  3. Possibly a change for some variables. The new value of **x** is denoted by **x'**, following **do**, for instance **do {x'=3, y'=0, z'<2}**.
  4. The target state: **goto lower**.

17.4 System Analysis

The analysis uses *instructions*. Actually, HYTECH contains a small interpreter to evaluate expressions representing unions of regions (See section 5.5).

The primitives consist in standard set operations, computation of successor and predecessor sets and some basic control instructions. (Such an evaluation takes place in the particular context of a given automaton system.)

A few instructions can thus be used to describe a (symbolic) computation of a set of configurations, for which a given property holds. In a way, HYTECH can be viewed as a programming language, allowing the user himself to build a symbolic model checking computation from the primitives (data structures and basic algorithms on regions).

Clearly, this provides a very flexible approach, but on the other hand, it requires some expertise from the user.

Regions computations. We first introduce some region variables, for later use:

```
var init, access, err: region;
```

Atomic propositions are constraints on the variable values and on the control states of the system components. The main operations are the following:

- boolean combinations : complementation (˜), union (|) and intersection (&) of regions. In the case of the railway crossing (where **x** is the clock of the train), the initial region is defined by:

```
init := loc[train]=far & x=0 & loc[gate]=up & a=90;
```

- convex hull computation;
- existential quantification (instruction **hide...endhide**);
- functions **pre** and **post**, which respectively compute the sets of immediate predecessors and successors;
- function **reach**, which computes the set of iterated successors (or predecessors) of a set of configurations. It is then possible to obtain both forward and backward analysis. For instance, the instruction:

```
access := reach forward from init endreach;
```

computes the set **access** of configurations reachable from the initial state **init**.

Safety properties. In order to check that the gate is closed when the train is inside the crossing, the set of configurations describing an error of the system is written in HYTECH as:

```
err := (loc[train]=on) & (~(loc[gate]=down));
```

We then have to compute the set of accessible states which are also an error state. The system is correct if the intersection of `access` and `err` is empty. Thus, the final analysis instruction is just an emptiness test.

```
prints "safety property";
if empty(access & err)
        then prints "ok";
        else prints "nok";
endif;
```

The result is the following:

```
Checking automaton gate
Checking automaton train
Composing automata *
.......Number of iterations required for reachability: 7

safety property
ok
```

Execution traces. Some functions in HYTECH provide paths in the region graph, thus allowing the user to obtain error diagnostics.

For instance, let us suppose we want to modify the railway crossing system with a train that arrives faster. We replace the value 10 by 4. In this case, the safety property becomes false and we want an example of an execution leading to an error state.

We only have to define an additional **region** variable R and change the final test:

```
R := access & err;
if empty(R)
        then prints "ok";
        else prints "nok";
        print trace to R using access;
endif;
```

The new result (from line 4) is now:

```
........Number of iterations required for reachability: 8

safety property
nok
 ====== Generating trace to specified target region ========
Time: 0.00
Location: far.up
    x = 0   & a = 90
```

```
----------------------------------
  VIA: app
----------------------------------
Time: 0.00
Location: near.lower
     x = 0    & a = 90
----------------
  VIA 6.00 time units
----------------
Time: 6.00
Location: near.lower
     x = 6    & a = 0
----------------------------------
  VIA:
----------------------------------
Time: 6.00
Location: on.lower
     x = 6    & a = 0
============= End of trace generation =============
```

17.5 Parametric Analysis

Parametric analysis is a specific and very interesting feature of HYTECH.

When a system (or a property) contains parameters, the analysis can provide the parameter values for which the property holds.

A parametric train. In the example above, let us suppose we know how long it takes for the gate to get open or closed, and we want to find the maximal amount of time for the train to enter the crossing, such that the system remains correct. To answer this question, we introduce a parameter m representing this amount of time (see figure 17.2).

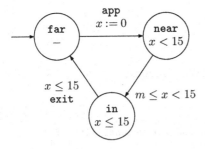

Fig. 17.2. Train with parameterized entry delay

The declarations of variables and train automaton now become:

```
var     a : analog;
        x : clock;
        m : parameter;

define(max,15)

automaton train
synclabs: app, exit;
initially far & a=90 & x=0;

loc far: while True wait {}
        when True sync app do {x'= 0} goto near;

loc near: while x < max wait {}
        when x >= m & x < max goto on;

loc on: while x <= max wait {}
        when x <= max goto far;

end -- train
```

Note that it is also possible to define constant values, like in define(max,15), thus avoiding painful replacements in the description file. The value of a constant is replaced before execution, while a parameter is handled in a symbolic way.

Analysis. We now have to compute the set of values of m for which the safety property does not hold. For this, we modify once more the final test:

```
if empty(R)
        then prints "ok";
        else prints "nok";
        prints "parameter values:";
        print omit all locations
                hide non_parameters in R endhide;
endif;
```

The instruction hide non_parameters in R endhide is an existential quantification, which computes a projection of region R, thus " hiding " all variables of the system except parameter m. We finally apply the operation omit all locations, which computes the disjunction of the constraints on the locations, yielding the expected result:

```
.........Number of iterations required for reachability: 9

safety property
```

```
nok
parameter values:
    m <= 6
```

We can conclude that the system is correct if and only if the maximal delay m is (strictly) greater than 6.

17.6 Documentation and Case Studies

HYTECH user's manual, *A user guide to* HYTECH, is available on the web page mentioned at the beginning. It is 41 pages long and describes the model, the analysis method, the basic instructions, examples and advice for installation and use. A short version appears in [HHW97].

There are many case studies, among which:

- a gas burner, a water level controller [ACHH93];
- a billiard, a temperature regulator for a nuclear plant [NOSY93];
- Fischer's mutual exclusion protocol, the railway crossing, a scheduler [AHH96, HHW95];
- a robot controller, Corbett's distributed control system, a parametric system [HH95b];
- Philips audio-control protocol [HW95];
- non-linear problems [HH95a, HW96a];
- the steam-boiler control [HW96b].

HyTech Bibliography

[ACHH93] R. Alur, C. Courcoubetis, T. A. Henzinger, and Pei-Hsin Ho. Hybrid automata: an algorithmic approach to the specification and verification of hybrid systems. In *Proc. Workshop Hybrid Systems, Lyngby, DK, Oct. 1992*, volume 736 of *Lecture Notes in Computer Science*, pages 209–229. Springer, 1993.

[AHH96] R. Alur, T. A. Henzinger, and Pei-Hsin Ho. Automatic symbolic verification of embedded systems. *IEEE Transactions on Software Engineering*, 22(3):181–201, 1996.

[HH95a] T. A. Henzinger and Pei-Hsin Ho. Algorithmic analysis of nonlinear hybrid systems. In *Proc. 7th Int. Conf. Computer Aided Verification (CAV'95), Liège, Belgium, July 1995*, volume 939 of *Lecture Notes in Computer Science*, pages 225–238. Springer, 1995.

[HH95b] T. A. Henzinger and Pei-Hsin Ho. HYTECH: The Cornell HYbrid TECHnology tool. In *Proc. Hybrid Systems II, Ithaca, NY, USA, Oct. 1994*, volume 999 of *Lecture Notes in Computer Science*, pages 265–293. Springer, 1995.

[HHW95] T. A. Henzinger, Pei-Hsin Ho, and H. Wong-Toi. HYTECH: the next generation. In *Proc. 16th IEEE Real-Time Systems Symposium (RTSS'95), Pisa, Italy, Dec. 1995*, pages 56–65. IEEE Comp. Soc. Press, 1995.

[HHW97] T. A. Henzinger, Pei-Hsin Ho, and H. Wong-Toi. HyTech: a model checker for hybrid systems. *Journal of Software Tools for Technology Transfer*, 1(1–2):110–122, 1997.

[HW95]   T. A. Henzinger and H. Wong-Toi. Automated analysis of an audio control protocol. In *Proc. Hybrid Systems II, Ithaca, NY, USA, Oct. 1994*, volume 999 of *Lecture Notes in Computer Science*, pages 265–293. Springer, 1995.

[HW96a] T. A. Henzinger and H. Wong-Toi. Linear phase-portrait approximations for nonlinear hybrid systems. In *Proc. Workshop Hybrid Systems III: Verification and Control, New Brunswick, NJ, USA, Oct. 1995*, volume 1066 of *Lecture Notes in Computer Science*, pages 377–388. Springer, 1996.

[HW96b] T. A. Henzinger and H. Wong-Toi. Using HyTech to synthesize control parameters for a steam boiler. In *Formal methods for industrial applications: specifying and programming the steam boiler control*, volume 1165 of *Lecture Notes in Computer Science*, pages 265–282. Springer, 1996.

[NOSY93] X. Nicollin, A. Olivero, J. Sifakis, and S. Yovine. An approach to the description and analysis of hybrid systems. In *Proc. Workshop Hybrid Systems, Lyngby, DK, Oct. 1992*, volume 736 of *Lecture Notes in Computer Science*, pages 149–178. Springer, 1993.

Main Bibliography

[ACD93]   R. Alur, C. Courcoubetis, and D. Dill. Model-checking in dense real-time. *Information and Computation*, 104(1):2–34, 1993.

[ACH⁺95] R. Alur, C. Courcoubetis, N. Halbwachs, T. A. Henzinger, Pei-Hsin Ho, X. Nicollin, A. Olivero, J. Sifakis, and S. Yovine. The algorithmic analysis of hybrid systems. *Theoretical Computer Science*, 138(1):3–34, 1995.

[ACHH93] R. Alur, C. Courcoubetis, T. A. Henzinger, and Pei-Hsin Ho. Hybrid automata: an algorithmic approach to the specification and verification of hybrid systems. In *Proc. Workshop Hybrid Systems, Lyngby, DK, Oct. 1992*, volume 736 of *Lecture Notes in Computer Science*, pages 209–229. Springer, 1993.

[AD94]   R. Alur and D. L. Dill. A theory of timed automata. *Theoretical Computer Science*, 126(2):183–235, 1994.

[ADS86]   B. Alpern, A. J. Demers, and F. B. Schneider. Safety without stuttering. *Information Processing Letters*, 23(4):177–180, 1986.

[AN82]   A. Arnold and M. Nivat. Comportements de processus. In *Actes du Colloque AFCET " Les Mathématiques de l'Informatique "*, pages 35–68, 1982.

[Arn92]   A. Arnold. *Systèmes de transitions finis et sémantique des processus communicants*. Collection Études et Recherches en Informatique. Masson, Paris, 1992.

[AS85]   B. Alpern and F. B. Schneider. Defining liveness. *Information Processing Letters*, 21(4):181–185, 1985.

[AS87]   B. Alpern and F. B. Schneider. Recognizing safety and liveness. *Distributed Computing*, 2:117–126, 1987.

[BCG88]   M. C. Browne, E. M. Clarke, and O. Grumberg. Characterizing finite Kripke structures in propositional temporal logic. *Theoretical Computer Science*, 59(1–2):115–131, 1988.

[BCM⁺92] J. R. Burch, E. M. Clarke, K. L. McMillan, D. L. Dill, and L. J. Hwang. Symbolic model checking: 10^{20} states and beyond. *Information and Computation*, 98(2):142–170, 1992.

[Bry86]   R. E. Bryant. Graph-based algorithms for boolean function manipulation. *IEEE Transactions on Computers*, C-35(8):677–691, 1986.

[Bry92]   R. E. Bryant. Symbolic boolean manipulation with ordered binary-decision diagrams. *ACM Computing Surveys*, 24(3):293–318, 1992.

[CBM90]   O. Coudert, C. Berthet, and J. C. Madre. Verification of synchronous sequential machines based on symbolic execution. In *Proc. Int. Workshop Automatic Verification Methods for Finite State Systems (CAV'89), Grenoble, June 1989*, volume 407 of *Lecture Notes in Computer Science*, pages 365–373. Springer, 1990.

[CE81]   E. M. Clarke and E. A. Emerson. Design and synthesis of synchronization skeletons using branching time temporal logic. In *Proc. Logics of*

Programs Workshop, Yorktown Heights, New York, May 1981, volume 131 of *Lecture Notes in Computer Science*, pages 52–71. Springer, 1981.

[CES86]   E. M. Clarke, E. A. Emerson, and A. P. Sistla. Automatic verification of finite-state concurrent systems using temporal logic specifications. *ACM Transactions on Programming Languages and Systems*, 8(2):244–263, 1986.

[CGL94a] E. Clarke, O. Grumberg, and D. Long. Verification tools for finite-state concurrent systems. In *A Decade of Concurrency, Proc. REX School/Symp., Noordwijkerhout, NL, June 1993*, volume 803 of *Lecture Notes in Computer Science*, pages 124–175. Springer, 1994.

[CGL94b] E. M. Clarke, O. Grumberg, and D. E. Long. Model checking and abstraction. *ACM Transactions on Programming Languages and Systems*, 16(5):1512–1542, 1994.

[CMP92]   E. Chang, Z. Manna, and A. Pnueli. Characterization of temporal property classes. In *Proc. 19th Int. Coll. Automata, Languages, and Programming (ICALP'92), Vienna, Austria, July 1992*, volume 623 of *Lecture Notes in Computer Science*, pages 474–486. Springer, 1992.

[Cou96]   P. Cousot. Abstract interpretation. *ACM Computing Surveys*, 28(2):324–328, 1996.

[CPS93]   R. Cleaveland, J. Parrow, and B. Steffen. The Concurrency Workbench: A semantics-based tool for the verification of concurrent systems. *ACM Transactions on Programming Languages and Systems*, 15(1):36–72, 1993.

[DGG97]   D. Dams, R. Gerth, and O. Grumberg. Abstract interpretation of reactive systems. *ACM Transactions on Programming Languages and Systems*, 19(2):111–149, 1997.

[DV90]   R. De Nicola and F. Vaandrager. Action versus state based logics for transition systems. In *Semantics of Systems of Concurrent Processes: LITP Spring School on Theoretical Computer Science, La Roche Posay, France, Apr. 1990*, volume 469 of *Lecture Notes in Computer Science*, pages 407–419. Springer, 1990.

[EC80]   E. A. Emerson and E. M. Clarke. Characterizing correctness properties of parallel programs using fixpoints. In *Proc. 7th Coll. Automata, Languages and Programming (ICALP'80), Noordwijkerhout, NL, Jul. 1980*, volume 85 of *Lecture Notes in Computer Science*, pages 169–181. Springer, 1980.

[EH82]   E. A. Emerson and J. Y. Halpern. Decision procedures and expressiveness in the temporal logic of branching time. In *Proc. 14th ACM Symp. Theory of Computing (STOC'82), San Francisco, CA, May 1982*, pages 169–180, 1982.

[EH86]   E. A. Emerson and J. Y. Halpern. "Sometimes" and "Not Never" revisited: On branching versus linear time temporal logic. *Journal of the ACM*, 33(1):151–178, 1986.

[EL87]   E. A. Emerson and Chin-Laung Lei. Modalities for model checking: Branching time logic strikes back. *Science of Computer Programming*, 8(3):275–306, 1987.

[Eme90]   E. A. Emerson. Temporal and modal logic. In J. van Leeuwen, editor, *Handbook of Theoretical Computer Science, vol. B*, chapter 16, pages 995–1072. Elsevier Science, 1990.

[GPSS80] D. Gabbay, A. Pnueli, S. Shelah, and J. Stavi. On the temporal analysis of fairness. In *Proc. 7th ACM Symp. Principles of Programming Languages (POPL'80), Las Vegas, NV, USA, Jan. 1980*, pages 163–173, 1980.

[Hen96]   T. A. Henzinger. The theory of hybrid automata. In *Proc. 11th IEEE Symp. Logic in Computer Science (LICS'96), New Brunswick, NJ, USA, July 1996*, pages 278–292, 1996.

[HKPV98]   T. A. Henzinger, P. W. Kopke, A. Puri, and P. Varaiya. What's decidable about hybrid automata? *Journal of Computer and System Sciences*, 57(1):94–124, 1998.

[Kam68]   J. A. W. Kamp. *Tense Logic and the theory of linear order*. PhD thesis, UCLA, Los Angeles, CA, USA, 1968.

[Kin94]   E. Kindler. Safety and liveness properties: A survey. *EATCS Bull.*, 53:268–272, 1994.

[Kos82]   S. R. Kosaraju. Decidability of reachability in vector addition systems. In *Proc. 14th ACM Symp. Theory of Computing (STOC'82), San Francisco, CA, May 1982*, pages 267–281, 1982.

[Koy90]   R. Koymans. Specifying real-time properties with metric temporal logic. *Real-Time Systems*, 2(4):255–299, 1990.

[Koz83]   D. Kozen. Results on the propositional μ-calculus. *Theoretical Computer Science*, 27(3):333–354, 1983.

[Lam73]   L. Lamport. Proving the correctness of multiprocess programs. *IEEE Transactions on Software Engineering*, 3(2):125–143, 1973.

[LP85]   O. Lichtenstein and A. Pnueli. Checking that finite state concurrent programs satisfy their linear specification. In *Proc. 12th ACM Symp. Principles of Programming Languages (POPL'85), New Orleans, LA, USA, Jan. 1985*, pages 97–107, 1985.

[LS85]   L. Lamport and F. B. Schneider. Formal foundation for specification and verification. In *Distributed systems: methods and tools for specification: an advanced course*, volume 190 of *Lecture Notes in Computer Science*, pages 203–285. Springer, 1985.

[LS95]   F. Laroussinie and Ph. Schnoebelen. A hierarchy of temporal logics with past. *Theoretical Computer Science*, 148(2):303–324, 1995.

[May84]   E. W. Mayr. An algorithm for the general Petri net reachability problem. *SIAM J. Comput.*, 13(3):441–460, 1984.

[Mil89]   R. Milner. *Communication and Concurrency*. Prentice Hall Int., 1989.

[MP90]   Z. Manna and A. Pnueli. A hierarchy of temporal properties. In *Proc. 9th ACM Symp. Principles of Distributed Computing (PODC'90), Quebec City, Canada, Aug. 1990*, pages 377–408, 1990.

[Pap94]   C. H. Papadimitriou. *Computational Complexity*. Addison-Wesley, 1994.

[Pet81]   G. L. Peterson. Myths about the mutual exclusion problem. *Information Processing Letters*, 12(3):115–116, 1981.

[Pix92]   C. Pixley. A theory and implementation of sequential hardware equivalence. *IEEE Transactions on Computer-Aided Design of Integrated Circuits*, 11(12):1469–1478, 1992.

[Pnu77]   A. Pnueli. The temporal logic of programs. In *Proc. 18th IEEE Symp. Foundations of Computer Science (FOCS'77), Providence, RI, USA, Oct.-Nov. 1977*, pages 46–57, 1977.

[Pnu81]   A. Pnueli. The temporal semantics of concurrent programs. *Theoretical Computer Science*, 13(1):45–60, 1981.

[QS82]   J.-P. Queille and J. Sifakis. Specification and verification of concurrent systems in CESAR. In *Proc. Int. Symp. on Programming, Turin, Italy, Apr. 1982*, volume 137 of *Lecture Notes in Computer Science*, pages 337–351. Springer, 1982.

[Reu89]   C. Reutenauer. *Aspects Mathématiques des Réseaux de Petri*. Collection études et recherches en informatique. Masson, Paris, 1989.

[Sis85]   A. P. Sistla. On characterization of safety and liveness properties in temporal logic. In *Proc. 4th ACM Symp. Principles of Distributed Computing (PODC'85), Minaki, ON, Canada, Aug. 1985*, pages 39–48, 1985.

[Sis94]   A. P. Sistla. Safety, liveness and fairness in temporal logic. *Formal Aspects of Computing*, 6(5):495–512, 1994.

[Tho90]   W. Thomas. Automata on infinite objects. In J. van Leeuwen, editor, *Handbook of Theoretical Computer Science, vol. B*, chapter 4, pages 133–191. Elsevier Science, 1990.

[Var96]   M. Y. Vardi. An automata-theoretic approach to linear temporal logic. In *Logics for Concurrency: Structure Versus Automata*, volume 1043 of *Lecture Notes in Computer Science*, pages 238–266. Springer, 1996.

[VC92]   G. Vidal-Naquet and A. Choquet-Geniet. *Réseaux de Petri et Systèmes Parallèles*. Armand Colin, 1992.

[VW86]   M. Vardi and P. Wolper. An automata-theoretic approach to automatic program verification. In *Proc. 1st IEEE Symp. Logic in Computer Science (LICS'86), Cambridge, MA, USA, June 1986*, pages 332–344, 1986.

Index